Euripides

Alcestis
Medea
Hippolytus

Euripides

Alcestis
Medea
Hippolytus

Translated by Diane Arnson Svarlien

Introduction and Notes by Robin Mitchell-Boyask

Hackett Publishing Company, Inc.
Indianapolis/Cambridge

12 11 10 09 08 07   1 2 3 4 5 6 7

For further information, please address:

Hackett Publishing Company, Inc.
P.O. Box 44937
Indianapolis, IN 46244-0937

www.hackettpublishing.com

Cover design by Brian Rak and Abigail Coyle
Text design by Meera Dash
Maps by William Nelson
Composition by William Hartman
Printed at Edwards Brothers, Inc.

Library of Congress Cataloging-in-Publication Data

Euripides.
    [Selections. English. 2007]
    Alcestis, Medea, Hippolytus / Euripides; translated by Diane Arnson
Svarlien; introduction and notes by Robin Mitchell-Boyask.
        p. cm.
    Includes bibliographical references.
    ISBN 978-0-87220-822-3 (pbk.)—ISBN 978-0-87220-823-0 (cloth)
    1. Euripides—Translations into English. 2. Alcestis (Greek
mythology)—Drama. 3. Medea (Greek mythology)—Drama.
4. Hippolytus (Greek mythology)—Drama. 5. Mythology, Greek—
Drama. I. Arnson Svarlien, Diane, 1960– II. Mitchell-Boyask,
Robin, 1961– III. Title.

PA3975.A2 2007
882'.01—dc22

                                                          2007015305

Contents

Introduction

The works featured in this volume—three major plays of the Athenian dramatist Euripides—date from the years 438–428 BCE, the third decade of the dramatist's career, though only the first from which any of his dramas survive. Born sometime around 480 BCE, Euripides first entered the dramatic contest at the City Dionysia (also known as the Festival of Dionysus) in 455. His debut program included *The Daughters of Pelias*, a drama that depicted the murder of King Pelias by his daughters at the urging of the duplicitous barbarian princess Medea, then still desperate to assist her new husband, Jason. This play showed the new dramatist already exploring such issues as gender, marriage, ethnicity, and intrafamilial violence while demonstrating an almost lurid fascination with the more unseemly aspects of Greek myth. These themes would resurface throughout Euripides' career, not least in *Alcestis, Medea,* and *Hippolytus,* and perhaps most fully in an extant drama he left unproduced at his death in 406, the *Bacchae*. While the dramas included in this volume are among the first of the surviving works of Euripides, they are nonetheless products of a mature artist. They were moreover created at a crucial moment in Athenian history by a keen observer of that moment, an artist who passed from his early forties into his fifties as his home city of Athens moved from an almost unquestioned dominance of the political and cultural life of the Greek world to the early years of the Peloponnesian War against its rival city-state, Sparta.

Despite their production over a ten-year period, these three dramas have a remarkable amount in common, even at the most mundane level: we know, for example, the exact year in which each was produced at the City Dionysia (about which, more later). Further, the myths that provide the plots of all three are set in the generation before the Trojan War. None of them feature a dialogue among three characters, although one can see Euripides grasping in that direction in the last scene of *Hippolytus*. Each examines the trials and tribulations of marriage and the particular problems encountered by Greek (and, perhaps, all) wives and mothers, including the fate of children once their birth mother is gone. In

Medea and *Alcestis,* a woman is the main character, and the title of *Hippolytus* should not obscure the prominence of Phaedra; she has almost as many lines as the title character, and the poignancy of her situation has prompted some critics to argue that Phaedra, not Hippolytus, is the true tragic figure in that play. I shall explore all of these matters in the pages that follow. First I shall examine the relationship between Euripides and the Athens of his time, then the nature of the City Dionysia and Euripides' participation in it, and, finally, the three dramas themselves.

Euripides and Athens in the Fifth Century

Euripides' life coincided with the span of almost the entire fifth century BCE, an era of breathtaking change in nearly every aspect of Greek life. That his dramas interact with these transformations and with the sheer level of agitation in Athenian society during that century's later decades probably accounts for much of the fascination with Euripides in our era, which has seen a comparable level of upheaval. The seeming modernity of Euripides, however, has fed into some stereotypes fostered by Euripides' contemporary, the comic poet Aristophanes, who mercilessly lampooned Euripides in a number of plays: by name in *Clouds,* and by making him a character in *Acharnians, Women at the Thesmophoria,* and, last but not least, *Frogs.* Aristophanes constantly mocked Euripides as the decadent purveyor of all cultural trends, a follower of the Sophists, an atheist, and an excessively bookish poet who staged fallen women and ruined heroes in rags. These comic dramas are largely responsible for Euripides' notoriety in subsequent centuries, and they certainly present caricatures, but since they also tap into the dynamic energy that circulated between Euripidean drama and the city of Athens in the fifth century, Aristophanes' portrayal of Euripides is a good starting point for this subject.

From his earliest surviving comedies to the first written after the death of Euripides, Aristophanes stressed the modern, revolutionary, and democratic aspects of Euripides and his dramas. He ridiculed both Euripides' artistic style and the content of his plots. In the first surviving comic drama, *Acharnians,* Aristophanes' hero Dicaeopolis needs to adopt a sympathetic—actually, pathetic—persona in order to defend himself against the hostile Acharnians, who are furious with him because of his personal truce with the Spartans. It occurs to him that Euripides must have an abundant supply of ragged beggar costumes, and so he visits the playwright while the latter is hard at work in his library (an unusual possession at that time, and perhaps one of the few details of Euripidean legend that was true). Euripides provides Dicaeopolis with the costume of Telephus, whose story of an outcast, wounded hero formed the basis of one of Euripides' plays in 438, thirteen years before *Acharnians* (and as part of the same program as *Alcestis*). Dicaeopolis then adopts not just the clothes but also the situation of Telephus in a scene parodying Euripides' tragedy, whose hilarity is especially remarkable because the tragic model is lost to us.

Two years later, in Aristophanes' *Clouds*, Strepsiades falls into a violent dispute with his son Pheidippides because junior refuses to sing a song from a drama by that paragon of virtue, Aeschylus. The father asks, "Why don't you come up with some of that clever modern stuff, something from one of those fashionable poets you're always going on about?" In response, Pheidippides "blurt[s] out some disgusting lines from Euripides, about a brother and sister going at it together!" Strepsiades reacts with dismay, and so his son in turn beats his father because he "dared to insult a gifted man like Euripides."[1] Euripides is thus represented as the flash point for the burgeoning generation gap in Athens during the 420s.

Euripides returns as a character a dozen years later in *Women at the Thesmophoria* of 411. The Thesmophoria was an Athenian festival in honor of the goddess Demeter, during which women removed themselves from men for a period of three days and camped out, possibly in (of all places) the Pnyx, the meeting place of the Athenian Assembly. In Aristophanes' comedy, the women of Athens take advantage of their conclave to plot violence against Euripides because he has slandered them repeatedly in his plays. On the surface, this seems grossly unfair, for while he does depict one woman as murderous in *Medea* and another in the throes of adulterous, quasi-incestuous, passion in *Hippolytus*, he still depicts their motivations and situations with insightful sympathy. Moreover, there are very few women in Greek theater as unambiguously noble as Alcestis. Yet Euripides' choice to recast heroic legend in terms of gender conflicts and domestic intrigue opened the door to the kinds of parodic simplifications that generate comedy in any

---

1. Aristophanes, *Clouds*, translated by Peter Meineck (Indianapolis: Hackett Publishing, 2000), lines 1368–77.

era. As Euripides attempts to escape injury or even death at the hands of these angry women, Aristophanes engages in a wild burlesque of two of Euripides' plays: his now lost *Andromeda* and his *Helen,* which fortunately does survive.

The most telling portrayal of Euripides in Aristophanes comes six years later in *Frogs,* at a time when Athens was in the last desperate months of its long struggle with Sparta, and the city's sense of impending doom was heightened by the deaths of its most prominent tragic poets: Sophocles a few months earlier, and Euripides during the previous year, most likely during his self-imposed exile in the court of the king of Macedonia. Sophocles, an ancient source records, dressed himself in black for the Proagon, a preliminary ceremony at the City Dionysia, and brought his chorus in without garlands after news of his colleague's death had reached him. In Aristophanes' comedy, the god Dionysus mourns the death of Euripides and recognizes that none of the remaining poets are up to the job of entertaining and educating the citizens of Athens, and so he descends to the Underworld to retrieve Euripides. Yet, upon his arrival, Aeschylus (who had died half a century before) and Euripides are fighting over the title of greatest playwright among the dead, and Dionysus is drawn into the struggle to such an extent that he presides over a contest between the two, with the winner allowed to return to the living with him. Aeschylus again is cast as the defender of the good old days and their good old ways, and Euripides as the decadent modernist. Nevertheless, Aeschylus himself is depicted as a pompous, often incomprehensible windbag, and the portrayal of a Euripides who "democratizes" high tragedy by allowing more realistic and lower-class characters is fair and generally on the mark. The competition affords opportunities for much silliness, yet a more sober thought recurs throughout, namely, that tragic poets have something to teach their city, that they make citizens better in some way. In the end, Euripides trips over his own sophistic witticisms and Dionysus chooses Aeschylus, who exits giving the strict command that Sophocles, not Euripides, should take his throne in the Underworld. Poor Euripides is thus defeated among both the living and the dead.

The form of Dionysus' response to Euripides' protest at his abandonment is a perfect example of the problems Aristophanes saw in Euripidean drama. Let us look at the passage (1469–75, my translation):

EUR.: Remember now the oaths you swore to the gods
     that you'd take me back home. Choose your friends!

DIO.: "My tongue is bound by oath . . ." I shall choose Aeschylus.

EUR.: What have you done, most foul of men?

DIO.: Me? I decided that Aeschylus wins. Why not?

EUR.: You can look me in the face when you've done a most
     shameful deed?

DIO.: "But what is shameful, unless it seems so to those who
     watch?"

Dionysus here throws two notorious Euripidean quotations back at
their author (and even piles on a third in a response that follows the
passage quoted above). Throughout all of these comic dramas, Aristophanes harps on the sophistic witticisms and the self-consciously
rhetorical style of the speakers in the dramas of Euripides, who
was so clearly and deeply affected by the flowering of the teaching
of rhetoric in Athens by the Sophists during his lifetime in a way
that Sophocles, older by a decade, was not; while Sophoclean
characters certainly often reflect the more formalized style of
speech that was gaining popularity, they never sound so much like
lawyers or (bad) politicians as Jason does in defending himself
against Medea or Hippolytus against his father, Theseus. The last
line in the passage quoted above is an adaptation of Euripides' lost
Aeolus and its original version, which ended "to those who do," is
said to have shocked the Athenians, as did possibly the line from
Hippolytus, "My tongue is bound by oath, but not my mind"
(673).[2] Sophistry, Aristophanes seems to suggest here, ultimately
defeats itself. And while the *Hippolytus* quotation, taken out of
context, is unfair to Euripides, since Hippolytus is destroyed
because he *does not* violate his oath, it is easy to imagine such
memorable lines being bandied about the streets of Athens and at
evening drinking parties (*symposia*) where reciting poetry was one
of the main activities.

    Yet Aristophanes surely realized that Euripides was more the
mirror reflecting the changes in society than the lamp lighting their
way. Euripides' willingness to represent these changes and to depict

---

2. All line references to plays in this volume are to Arnson Svarlien's
translation.

heroes with the same problems, challenges, and speech as normal people, in a volatile mixture of myth and social realism—*that*, for Aristophanes, was the real issue. Aristotle, it is useful to recall here, preserves in *Poetics* 1460b35 Sophocles' observation that he himself "portrayed people the way they ought to be and Euripides the way they are." Thus in the three plays in this volume, we see the typical, mundane feminine concerns of Medea and Phaedra, the lethal pragmatism of the latter's Nurse, and the petty domestic squabbles inside the family of Admetus. The conflicts in all three plays are constantly cast in the rhetorical language and tactics taught by the Sophists, which had quickly taken over the courts and the Athenian Assembly and which had also been brought to bear on traditional morality; the Nurse's "second thoughts" about Phaedra's passion for her stepson Hippolytus are a prime example of the effects of such questioning. Euripides thus was simply too big and easy a target. And as social controversy is always the comedian's bread and butter, Aristophanes needed Euripidean innovation and extremity. It could be that some of the wilder flights of fancy in Aristophanes were inspired by Euripides' pushing the limits of what was possible in the tragic theater by increasingly incorporating comic elements into it. Aristophanes' relative neglect of Sophocles in *Frogs* suggests that it was difficult to make much comic fodder out of a person who was so universally admired and a poet who expressed a more traditional view of the norms of Greek society. Euripides, tired of losing to Sophocles and fed up with the ridicule from Aristophanes, departed for Macedonia at some point late in his life, perhaps after the production of his *Orestes* in 408; a failure in Athens, he was now to become a poet in the court of the king of Macedonia.

At least that is what some of the biographical stories would have us believe. Was Euripides really so unpopular in Athens? No. Much evidence suggests the opposite. In recent years, scholars have shown that many aspects of the received biographies of the ancient poets are false (see Lefkowitz 1981), and the image of the embittered poet, uttering views ahead of his time, exiled and then popular after his death has proven too appealing to resist. Indeed, Scullion (2003), who argues that the xenophobic comedy of Aristophanes would surely have seized upon any sojourn in Macedonia and run with it in *Frogs*, has recently questioned whether Euripides ever made the trip at all. And Aristophanes would not have continually picked on an individual who was not fundamentally prominent and popular. Further, Euripides seems to have had an enormous impact on Sophocles himself, as seen in the ruined heroes of his last two surviving dramas, *Philoctetes* and *Oedipus at Colonus*. Several decades after his death, Euripides was acclaimed by Aristotle, despite the philosopher's preference for Sophocles, as "the most tragic" of the poets. Moreover, two anecdotes from Plutarch in fact show that Euripides was more popular than a mere victory list would indicate. In the aftermath of Athens' disastrous expedition against Sicily (415–413 BCE), a group of surviving soldiers were given food and drink by their opponents after they sang some of Euripides' lyrics (Plutarch, *Nicias* 29). Plutarch continues that the grateful warriors, immediately upon their return to Athens, personally expressed their gratitude to their poetic savior. Plutarch's *Lysander* (15.3) preserves a story that, in 404, as Sparta debated the punishment of the now defeated Athens, its generals stopped their consideration of civic annihilation and enslavement when they heard a dinnertime performance of the first choral ode of Euripides' *Electra*: "They felt that it would be a barbarous act to annihilate a city that had produced such men." Now these later anecdotes might have been influenced by the heightened prestige of Euripides in the Hellenistic world (Plutarch lived in the first and second centuries CE), yet they ring reasonably true. But to understand that popularity and success can be seen very differently than anecdotal evidence might allow, we need to consider Euripides and the annual festival for which he composed his dramas, the City Dionysia.

Euripides and the City Dionysia

A resident of a modern city can see a performance of a drama most weeks, if not most nights of the year, and anyone anywhere can watch a movie whenever he or she wants. Obviously, an ancient Athenian did not make regular trips to the cinema, but theater was not part of his daily life, either. Aeschylus, Sophocles, and Euripides (and Aristophanes) wrote their dramas with the expectation that they would be performed a single time at the City Dionysia, the Athenian civic festival held annually in late March in honor of the god Dionysus. I say they wrote with this *expectation* because the actual frequency of production is often misunderstood and the scholarly view of this frequency is currently shifting. Aeschylus staged his Athenian dramas anew in Sicily, and it is unimaginable that Euripides, if his trip to Macedonia did occur, did not also produce his older works there. Moreover, sometime during the second half of the fifth century, posthumous productions of Aeschylean drama were allowed at the City Dionysia, so Euripides and Sophocles likely composed with this possibility in mind. Vase paintings from southern Italy frequently depict scenes from Athenian tragedy, which suggests that drama quickly became one of Athens' most popular exports. On the other hand, the Theater of Dionysus on the Acropolis was not the only theater in Attica (the term for greater Athens that included the surrounding countryside), and scholars increasingly tend to believe that poets, after productions at the City Dionysia, took their dramas on tour to the smaller theaters in the *demes,* the villages that constituted greater Athens. Nonetheless, the notional, if not actual, sole and "real" production was for the prestigious competitions of the City Dionysia.

And the Dionysia was extraordinarily competitive, with, among other things, many contests for choral groups from every tribe of Athens, and prizes for the best actors and, of course, for the tragic poet who produced the best slate of dramas, which consisted of three tragedies and a satyr play (described later in this Introduction). Well before each Dionysia, poets would apply for a chorus to the archon, the chief magistrate of Athens, who was in charge of all aspects of the festival. The central element in Greek drama was the chorus; because of its size (roughly fifteen for Euripides' career) and the complexity of its theatrical role, a chorus was very expensive to maintain and train for the months of rehearsals, so each one had to be supported by the city and its wealthy citizens. The criteria for the archon's selections remain unknown, though some evidence suggests that a particularly poor showing the previous year could jeopardize an applicant's chances. Because Aristotle's *Poetics* and Aristophanes' *Frogs* (not to mention other sources) name a number of other fifth-century playwrights, it is clear that Euripides would have had to vie for a chorus regularly. In other words, just as a bronze medal in the modern Olympics can obscure the many victories, both national and international, it can take just to reach the final race, so too a third-place finish at the Dionysia hardly suggests abject failure.

In such a competitive (the Greek term is *agonistic*) society, victory garnered its owner considerable glory and prestige, and it is highly unlikely that, in such an environment, disputes over the judging did not arise. Plutarch's *Life of Cimon* (8) tells a story that, when Sophocles won his first victory over Aeschylus, Cimon and several other generals were called on to adjudicate because the spectators had divided among themselves so passionately. The defeated Aeschylus is said to have left then for Sicily, never to return (an apocryphal story that the later production of Aeschylus' *Oresteia* belies). Again, these biographical details can be questioned, but the shape of the story does credibly suggest how high passions might have run. Euripides himself won first prize only three times during his life out of the twenty-two times he competed, and once posthumously (for the program that included the *Bacchae* and *Iphigenia at Aulis*), and human nature would suggest that this rate of success, in the face of Sophocles' eighteen victories, must have rankled him, especially since the events and their judging were so public. We do not know why he won so infrequently, but his stylistic innovations and plot choices probably contributed. It is difficult not to see Medea's complaint (304–12) about how clever people are held in suspicion and contempt as to some extent autobiographical. But one must keep in mind that Euripides did reach "the finals"—being thought worthy by the city to receive a chorus—twenty-two times. Many would gladly live with that kind of failure.

The years Euripides did receive a chorus from Athens, he would have participated fully in a most astonishing week of activities: among other events, he would have witnessed or engaged in parades, choral contests, displays of Athenian military power, presentations of civic honor, nine tragedies, three satyr plays, and a number of comedies. Here I summarize the excellent account of the Dionysia from Csapo and Slater's *The Context of Ancient Drama* (1995). All of these events took place at a spring festival in honor of the god Dionysus, a fertility deity who presided over the theater, but whose most prominent symbol was wine. The open-air Theater of Dionysus was located on the south slope of the Athenian Acropolis, a central location that itself indicated the importance of the theatrical festival. The City Dionysia was held in late March, the Athenian month of Elaphebolion, when the onset of milder weather and calmer seas allowed participation from all over the Mediterranean. On the eighth of Elaphebolion, the three poets who had been selected by the archon would appear in the Odeon (at least after its construction around 440), a roofed theater adjacent to the Theater of Dionysus. In the ceremony called the Proagon ("Before the Contest"), the poets would mount a stage, accompanied by their three actors and chorus, wearing garlands but without their costumes and masks. There they would speak about the dramas they were to perform in the coming days. The ninth of Elaphebolion was a day reserved for religious ceremonies, including a procession from the outskirts of Athens into the theater to commemorate the introduction of the god Dionysus to Attica. On the following day, official activities of the city were suspended and the festival began with a parade filled with representatives from all sectors of Athenian society. That same afternoon, there was a competition wherein each of the city's ten tribes would produce a chorus of fifty boys and another of fifty men to perform the choral works known as dithyrambs. As in the performances of tragic dramas, the choral groups would both sing and dance in honor of Dionysus. Thus, because every year 1,000 Athenians would compete in choruses even before the three days of tragic performances, the Theater of Dionysus would be filled with a large group of experts on choral performance, ready to find fault with or praise the choruses of the tragic dramas.

Our sources disagree about what happened on the succeeding days. Many believe that, beginning on the eleventh of Elaphebolion, a day with five comedies was followed by three days in which each of the approved poets would produce three tragedies and a satyr play; evidence suggests this was the arrangement before and after the Peloponnesian War (431–404 BCE), whose economic hardships likely reduced the number of comic dramas. Another theory is that there were five days of performances in which comedy and choral competitions were held for two, followed by three of tragedy and satyr plays. It is clear, however, that the competition began with a series of ceremonies, including a ritual cleansing of the theater, libations to the gods poured by generals, the awarding of golden crowns to prominent citizens who had helped the state during the previous year, a display of tribute silver sent by subject members of the Athenian alliance (less charitably called an empire), and the awarding of armor to orphaned sons of warriors who had died on behalf of Athens. All of this, and numerous sacrifices of animals, even before a single line was spoken by an actor! It is thus clear that the performance of Greek drama was woven into the fabric of Athenian society in a way that would be almost inconceivable for ours.

To someone of our own time, the most striking feature of each day of performance might have been the endurance required of both performers and audience. The performers Euripides had at his disposal for all of the four plays on his slate were three actors and a chorus of fifteen; shortly before Euripides' debut, Sophocles had been allowed to expand the number of actors from two to three. Those eighteen acted, danced, and sang from very early in the morning until well into the afternoon. Moreover, even within a single play, each actor had to take several roles, often of wildly different natures; for example, in Euripides' *Hippolytus,* the same actor played both Phaedra and her husband, Theseus. The simple, realistic masks that the actors donned for each part facilitated this practice. Some actors came to specialize in certain types of roles, especially those that required the ability to sing the lengthy complex solo arias that Euripides used more and more as his career progressed. The audience for each day of four plays likely arrived early, before sunrise, in order to secure the best seats possible on the stone and wood benches and up onto the bare slope above the theater itself. Roughly 15,000 Athenians and foreigners thus sat closely together, an arrangement that must have magnified their reactions to the emotionally charged events they watched below them. After performing three tragic dramas that represented love, death, murder, betrayal, and war, the chorus would return for the fourth dressed as satyrs, sexually excitable half-man, half-goat creatures, and engage in a burlesque of some sort, possibly parodying the tragedies that preceded them; like tragedy, the satyr dramas drew their plots from Greek mythology. While some need for comic relief after the three tragedies seems understandable, one would be hard-pressed to find an appropriate modern comparison. Perhaps *King Lear* followed by *Monty Python?* While only one pure satyr play survives, Euripides' *Cyclops,* one source tells us that *Alcestis* was performed in the place of a satyr play, a unique circumstance I shall discuss later.

Finally, after all of the ceremonies and performances, after the last satyr play on the third day of tragedies, the judges would make their decisions and the winners would be proclaimed before the assembled audience. The victors received a crown of ivy leaves, and then, accompanied by the *choregoi,* the wealthy individuals who had financed their choruses, they were led through the streets of Athens in yet another procession. Of the three dramas in this volume, only *Hippolytus* (and the three other dramas, now lost, on the same slate) afforded Euripides the chance for this extremely happy, and extremely public, celebration.

The Plays

Modern critical attempts to come to grips with Euripidean drama have proven no less contentious than ancient ones seem to have been. Each of these three dramas has been controversial among scholars, who have come to often startlingly different conclusions about the characters and their actions. My introduction to each drama will attempt to sketch out some of the primary points of controversy without excessively advocating one position over another. Readers who wish to pursue these arguments more fully are encouraged to consult the secondary readings listed at the back of this volume.

Aristophanes aside, quarrels over Euripides began in late-nineteenth-century Europe with Friedrich Nietzsche, who, though better known today as a philosopher, began his career as a classical philologist at the University of Basel. In his short book *The Birth of Tragedy* (1872), Nietzsche, then infatuated with the operas of Richard Wagner, argued that Greek tragedy had achieved a balance of the two primary forces in the human spirit, the Apollonian (the rational) and the Dionysian (the irrational), until Euripides, with his (alleged) devotion to the philosopher Socrates, tipped the scales in favor of science, thus destroying Greek tragedy. While many believe still that Nietzsche's basic insight into tragic drama was profound, it is difficult to see the author of *Hippolytus* and the *Bacchae* in these criticisms. Nietzsche was immediately, and violently, attacked by his classicist rival, the young Ulrich von Wilamowitz, who then, with a calmer head, proceeded to shape in a fundamental manner the modern study of ancient Greek literature; a defense of the tragedies of Euripides was an essential part of his scholarly career. But conflict has continued through several generations, as Ann Michelini has shown (in Mitchell-Boyask 2002, pp. 51–59). In general, Euripidean scholars advocate one of two main positions: either Euripides was an exponent of traditional Greek values and beliefs, or he was a radical who subjected all aspects of his society to a withering critique. *Alcestis, Medea,* and *Hippolytus* all seem to offer ammunition for both sides of this split. Admetus believes in the importance of social codes involving guests, and so he allows Heracles to stay in his house even though he is mourning his wife, Alcestis, who has died mere minutes before. Is Admetus therefore a noble man or an insensitive dolt who does not respect the memory of his wife, who has died on his behalf? Do the experiences of Medea expose the oppressiveness of patriarchal Greek culture, or do they affirm every negative Greek stereotype about women? Does the death of Hippolytus show the meaninglessness of devotion to the gods, or does it affirm their power and thus the necessity of proper worship? The arguments are as endless as they are rich.

Alcestis

The first extant work of Euripides (438 BCE), his *Alcestis,* seems at first glance charmingly simple, not least because it incorporates many folktale elements into its characters and plot, especially the motif of cheating death through a ruse. A woman dies so that her husband may live, and a great hero rescues her from the Underworld and restores her to her husband. Of course, a plot *that* simple would not make for compelling or challenging theater, so Euripides adds complexity with a well-meaning though self-absorbed, at times almost stupid, husband Admetus; a noble if perhaps ostentatious Alcestis whose motives in agreeing to die on behalf of her husband remain mysterious; and a magnanimous, not terribly perceptive, and inebriated hero Heracles. The shades of gray in these characters are sources of disagreement among readers of this drama. Is this a play about noble self-sacrifice, conjugal love, and the importance of traditional morality, or does it depict the cowardice and almost perfidious cluelessness of a husband who is bailed out only because his guest has superhuman powers?

The ambiguity of the genre to which *Alcestis* belongs contributes to the drama's interpretive elusiveness. Evidence suggests that *Alcestis* was performed in the place of a satyr drama, and hence it is commonly now called "prosatyric." An introduction to this work from the Hellenistic era reports some startling information about the productions of 438 at the City Dionysia: "First was Sophocles, and second was Euripides with *The Cretan Women, Alcmaeon, Telephus,* and *Alcestis. . . .* The drama has a rather comic conclusion." The introduction continues with some additional remarks on the "satyric" nature of Euripides' *Alcestis.* While we have enough fragments of *The Cretan Women* to know this drama was about the wild events leading to the birth of the Minotaur, and we have a clear sense of *Telephus* from Aristophanes' *Acharnians,* only *Alcestis* survives as a complete play from this program. No information exists as to how or why Euripides was allowed to substitute this play for the traditional ribald satyr drama to close his day of production, but this meager evidence does suggest that the rules of drama in Athens were more like guidelines than laws. The Chorus of *Alcestis* is not composed of satyrs, as would be the normal case for the fourth play on the program, but of old men, as is the case with many tragic dramas (e.g., Aeschylus' *Agamemnon* and Sophocles' *Antigone*). Yet, as our Hellenistic source observes, it is "rather like a satyr play because it turns against the tragic and toward joy and pleasure." These latter elements are clearly seen not just in the drama's happy ending, but in the humor that characterizes several scenes, including the banter between Apollo and Death and the intoxication of Heracles, a figure who was equally at home on the tragic and comic stages. It could also be that Euripides intended his audience to find humorous the spectacle of a man who does not realize that accepting the death of his wife in his place means that his wife will, in fact, be dead and he alive. Nevertheless, it is difficult to ignore the play's more serious aspects, such as the fears of Alcestis for her children's future and the violent dispute between Admetus and his father, Pheres.

With the drama thus poised between comedy and tragedy, Euripides is able to exploit his audience's conventional expectations and to construct a story whose trajectory, while still aiming toward a comic conclusion, nonetheless has moments of great sadness, even anguish, juxtaposed with the more humorous elements in an often unsettling manner. The audience initially sees the god Apollo emerge, youthful and resplendent, though potentially violent, with his characteristic bow and arrows. Admetus of Thessaly had earlier been kind to Apollo when Zeus punished the god with servitude to a mortal for killing the Cyclopes after Zeus destroyed Apollo's son Asclepius. The audience would have known that Asclepius, the founder of medicine, had angered Zeus by using his skills to resurrect a human being. Apollo has been helping Admetus to escape the day of death and explains Admetus' attempts to secure a volunteer to die in his place on the day assigned to him by the Fates. Death arrives and argues with Apollo about his mission. The rhetoric and legalisms of their debate are incongruous, probably humorously so, with the gravity of the situation, yet the clash provokes Apollo to prophesy the saving arrival of Heracles. After the Chorus begin to lament Alcestis and praise her as the "best of women," a servant continues to amplify the selfless nobility of

Alcestis in her preparations for death, while also introducing the
obtuseness of Admetus by reporting that he begs her not to leave
him. The Chorus continue their mourning as husband and wife
enter, but Euripides exploits his poetic resources to indicate further
that something is lacking in Admetus; Alcestis continually sings to
him in emotional lyrics, while Admetus replies in iambic trimeters,
the conversational rhythms of normal theatrical speech. The contrast is startling, and when Alcestis follows this exchange with an
extended speech that mixes a eulogy of herself with her fears for
her children by insisting that he never remarry, it is difficult not to
have the impression that she is disappointed in her husband. She
dies in full view of the audience, Admetus, and her children, who
then lament their mother in emotional lyrics while their father continues to respond in colorless, flat iambic trimeters. The Chorus
sing their wish that they could bring her back from Hades.

Enter Heracles, the greatest of all Greek heroes, instantly recog-
nizable to all with his lion-skin cloak (complete with head) and
club; if there is one man alive who could rescue Alcestis, it is this
hero who visits the Underworld with regularity in the course of his
heroic deeds. Here he is in the midst of his Twelve Labors in servitude to King Eurystheus (as Apollo had been, though in much
kinder circumstances, to Admetus), and Admetus now once again
goes out of his way to help a guest, again under extraordinary
conditions.

Admetus does so in adherence to a code of behavior known in
Greek as *xenia*, most commonly referred to now as the guest-host
relationship. *Xenia* was a sacred, reciprocal bond that guaranteed
the safety of travelers and those who sheltered them, and extended
even to their descendants. In Book 6 of Homer's *Iliad,* the Trojan
ally Glaucus and his Greek opponent Diomedes suddenly discover
they are ancestral guest-friends and, consequently, agree not to
fight but exchange armor instead. Many of the *Odyssey*'s social
relationships revolve around a series of encounters between guests
and hosts of varying levels of propriety. In Greek tragedy, many
characters find themselves in crises because of an excessive devotion to a particular value or virtue; for example, Hippolytus is
destroyed because his obsession with his chastity blots out all other
aspects of life. The dilemma of Admetus rests in being faced with a
guest, and an important one at that, immediately following the
death of his wife. Despite his public proclamations of devotion to
her memory, he immediately offers accommodation to Heracles

and lies to his guest when asked very pointed questions about the obvious signs of mourning. Many modern readers find this behavior inexplicable; indeed, members of the household of Admetus criticize him for his decision, and Heracles later seems genuinely upset about the deception. And yet, Admetus' determination to avoid discomfiting his guest impresses Heracles and moves him to take the initiative to rescue Alcestis from Death (885–910). The propriety of Admetus' zeal for *xenia* is perhaps the most contested issue of this drama. More problematic to some readers is Admetus' decision to accept the veiled woman Heracles brings to him in the play's final scene. The one request Alcestis makes of her husband is that he not take a new wife, and Admetus makes this promise in front of their children, which Alcestis duly notes. After wresting the body of Alcestis from Death, Heracles presents her, veiled, to Admetus and asks him to keep her safe. When Admetus demurs, it is on the grounds of public propriety, and not the promise he made to Alcestis. Heracles manages to convince Admetus that this is indeed his wife, but only after Admetus has agreed to accept her into his house. And is this in fact the same living wife Admetus buried? If so, what will she say to him later, given his behavior in this scene? And is not Death still owed a life if Alcestis has not in fact forfeited her life for her husband's? And why does she not speak? Whatever may explain her silence, it cannot be the simple fact that two speaking actors are already on stage.[3]

In trying to account for this silence, it is worth considering the possibility that Heracles may not be as truthful as he appears to be. He badly wants his friend to accept the woman, insisting that

---

3. Around two decades before the production of *Alcestis*, Sophocles had introduced the use of a third actor to the City Dionysia, Aeschylus' trilogic *Oresteia* being the first extant drama to use three. Although Euripides could have used as many as three speaking actors, *Alcestis* required only two, an option that would have involved the triple casting of the same actor as Alcestis, Pheres, and Heracles. In some dramas, such as Sophocles' *Ajax*, a character returns as played by a nonspeaking extra when all three speaking actors are occupied with other roles. In the case of a two-actor production of *Alcestis*, an additional speaking actor would of course have brought the total to only three, so the reason for Alcestis' silence in the final scene must be sought elsewhere. Scholars have recently argued that *Alcestis* was performed with three, not two, speaking actors, which invites that much more scrutiny of her silence. See Rehm (1994), p. 196, n. 48 for a full discussion.

Admetus not hear her voice for three days because she is still "consecrated to the gods below" (1207). That might be true, but it is also possible that Admetus' initial doubts about the identity of the woman are warranted, that the woman is not (or not exactly) who Heracles insists she is, and that Heracles and perhaps even the woman herself have an ulterior motive of some kind for wanting Admetus not to hear her voice for three days. Perhaps Heracles believes that three days will be long enough for Admetus to forget what his wife's voice actually sounds like, long enough to make it easier for Admetus to be permanently duped by either an impostor or a somehow changed Alcestis; three days may be long enough for a weak and pliable Admetus to become used to a woman who ultimately proves to be someone other than the wife he knew—and even to remarry, despite having promised Alcestis that he would not. In any event, much seems to hang on this silence, which neither Admetus nor we are allowed to hear broken at this crucial juncture.

Such ambiguity is characteristic of the close of this multifaceted drama, which resists attempts at overly simple readings. Even as Euripides invites his audience to anticipate the possibility that in three days Admetus may hear a voice that somehow discomfits him, he seems to suggest that there may be trouble ahead for Heracles, too—and indeed Heracles leaves the stage in quite a hurry; we must remember that Apollo had opened the drama with an allusion to the story of Asclepius, the son of a god who was destroyed for violating the line between the living and the dead, and the drama's end shows another son of a god returning a human from the Underworld, restored to life anew. Yet the lightness of Euripides' touch seems to ensure that such interpretive problems, like those of so many of his plays, will continue to defy definitive solutions.

Medea

So utterly opposite are this drama and its heroine to the earlier *Alcestis* that one might be tempted to suggest they were composed as a complementary pair had we not evidence to the contrary, as *Medea* was first produced seven years later, in 431 BCE, the moment when Athens and Sparta girded for war against each other. It is difficult not to imagine that the ferocity of this play's events is related to the tension of that time; a few months after the production of *Medea*, Spartan armies invaded the countryside of

Attica, plundering and burning their way to the city walls of Athens, a short walk from the Theater of Dionysus. The world of Athens was changing rapidly, and the savagery unleashed by Euripides in this tragedy seems prophetic of the violence and irrationality that would engulf his civilization in the coming years.

The kernel of this drama's plot, as with *Alcestis,* is simple—a wife's response to her husband's selfishness—and yet Euripides greatly complicates this scenario by making the wife a foreigner and then by continually varying the tone of the marital conflict and his audience's level of sympathy for each side from episode to episode and sometimes even from line to line. The folktale motif of the exotic princess who helps the handsome hero achieve his quest but is callously dispatched by him later is so prevalent in Greek myth that it must have been one of its older story types; Homer seems to play off the expectations of this type of story several times in the *Odyssey.* In Euripides' hands, the relationship has evolved so that the princess is now older, there are children, and the husband, his heroic career over, is dissatisfied with his lot in life. He does not leave her asleep on an island, as Theseus did to Ariadne, but simply takes a new wife, the daughter of the king of Corinth.

The upending of expectations is a fundamental part of Euripides' strategy in this drama. Jason's pursuit of the Golden Fleece had long been one of the central heroic myths of ancient Greece. Sent into exile as a child after Jason's uncle Pelias had deposed Jason's father, Jason had the typical hero's training by the centaur Chiron before returning to Iolcus to reclaim his patrimony. During his absence, he gained the favor of the goddess Hera who already hated Pelias. Pelias sent Jason off to fetch the fleece, officially to prove his worth, but really with the hope that he would not return from the dangerous journey to the Black Sea and the kingdom of Aeëtes, who kept the fleece guarded by a serpent. After assembling a crew of the greatest heroes of the generation before the Trojan War, including Heracles, Jason arrived in Colchis and requested the fleece from Aeëtes, who ordered him to first plow a field with fire-breathing bulls. Aeëtes' teenage daughter Medea, versed in the dark arts and already burning with love for the stranger, anointed his body with a protective oil against the bulls' fire and then put the guardian serpent to sleep. After escaping with the fleece, Medea and Jason killed her young brother, chopping his body to pieces and throwing them overboard in order to slow the pursuing fleet. Euripides' audience would have known this myth from an early though now lost epic, *Argonautica* (not to be confused with the Hellenistic epic by Apollonius of Rhodes), and from other poems such as Pindar's Fourth Pythian Ode. Euripides himself had dramatized aspects of this legend earlier in his career; as noted above, his very first entry in the City Dionysia included *The Daughters of Pelias*.

But nothing could have prepared his audience for what they saw in 431. As Edith Hall has shown, since the conclusion of the Persian Wars roughly a half-century earlier, Athens had fostered an image of itself as the defender of Greek values, and hence civilization itself, against the barbarians, whose quintessence was the Asiatic Persians, and Medea herself had become a useful symbol for the Persian threat to Greek manhood as embodied by Jason and Theseus. It is possible that the actor (and I stress actor, not actress) who played Medea (and only Medea) wore clothing of a distinctly Persian appearance and a mask that stressed her racial characteristics. A playwright perhaps had no greater challenge than centering a plot on this alien figure, and yet from the drama's opening lines we hear of the perfidy of Jason, the suffering of Medea, and the blind hostility of the Corinthian royal family. The drama thus explores the legitimacy of the Greek claim to superiority over barbarians. The Chorus of Corinthian women feel more solidarity and sympathy for Medea as a woman than contempt for her as a barbarian. Medea articulates to them the problems of marriage for women and the dangers they face in the process of childbirth in an extraordinary "feminist" speech that tempts us to forget that it was written by a man and spoken by a man to an audience composed largely, if not entirely, of men. Jason's self-presentation pushes the audience's sympathy further toward Medea as he talks in the style of a Sophist, full of flimsy, glib reasoning and legalisms. Moreover, as Bernard Knox (1979) observes, Medea's own language about herself is cast in the idioms of a Homeric warrior, obsessed with honor and with punishing enemies. Jason's despicable conduct overshadows whatever warning flags are raised by Medea's clear manipulation of the men she confronts and by the Nurse's fears about her dangerous intentions. Euripides manipulates his audience into a position of sympathy for his heroine as skillfully as she herself manipulates everyone who crosses her path.

Euripides then pulls the rug out from under his audience with Medea's decision to kill her children. King Aegeus stumbles in on his way home to Athens after consulting the Delphic oracle concerning his inability to sire children. His willingness to do anything to help Medea after she promises him assistance with his problem shows her how overwhelmingly important sons are to men; thus, she can inflict the maximum pain on Jason by depriving him of his legacy. She will murder Jason's new bride, and she knows that the codes of vengeance require that she pay a similar price. The Corinthians will kill her sons in response (Jason's first words in the last scene indicate she is correct in this assumption), so she must do it first. While the child-murdering Medea is now *the* Medea in our imagination, it is likely (though not universally agreed among scholars) that Euripides is the author who created this image; other ancient sources and the gradual way in which Euripides reveals this possibility both suggest a transformation of this myth to this most shocking form. Not only will Medea's actions lead to her children's deaths, but she herself will be the murderer and will break one of the most fundamental laws among humans and gods.

But where are the gods? Distant, it seems. Medea is a furious woman. Jason is a shadow of a hero, with not the least whiff of the semidivinity of Achilles or Heracles. He has broken his oaths to Medea, and oaths are sworn to, and thus guaranteed by, the gods. Jason, who pursues magical objects through fantastical means, seems like a hero from folktale rather than high myth, the realm to which Medea belongs. The Achillean rage of Medea transforms her into something more transcendent, perhaps a form of Hera, the goddess of marriage, the often-betrayed wife of Zeus who had earlier protected Jason but who is in this play nowhere to be seen. Perhaps Medea, in essence, becomes Hera. Anne Burnett (1973) has argued that Medea becomes a quasi-divine personification of the spirit that punishes oath breakers. Medea has continually told her audience that she does the work of the gods in punishing Jason. At the drama's close, she suddenly appears high above the stage, riding on the suspended platform, the space normally used for the gods who often appear late in a tragedy to resolve issues and denounce humans. She flies off to Athens on the dragon-drawn chariot of her grandfather, the sun god Helios. Jason cannot reach her, in either a literal or a figurative sense.

Medea has thus moved from being a sympathetic abused woman, to a monstrous child-killer, and finally to something almost indefinable and incomprehensible: a mother who kills her children and is not only unpunished but actually helped by the gods. Do the gods, then, care more about oaths than the lives of children? Is Euripides thus suggesting that the gods are amoral or, perhaps, ultimately false, uncaring, even unworthy of belief? Has Medea proven her heroic greatness in her punishment of Jason, or has she confirmed every stereotype about women and barbarians that has been articulated by the Greek men in the drama? These are some of the many questions raised at the drama's end. In the City Dionysia of 431, Euripides placed third out of three. I often wonder whether the sheer horror of the deliberate murders of the children had something to do with this defeat.

Hippolytus

Euripides' *Hippolytus* presents another story about the problems of women in Greek society and the marriage of mythical women to heroes. As in *Medea*, a foreign bride is taken to a Greek city and, as events unfold, a father is ultimately, though indirectly, responsible for a son's death. As in *Alcestis*, a wife is determined to do the right thing, to have a good reputation, and dies in the effort. Unlike in *Medea*, the gods are present, but the humans might wish they were not, for the gods display a terrifying combination of hostility and indifference to human suffering. A further connection with *Alcestis* is that the mortal whom Asclepius tried to resurrect was Hippolytus, a myth Euripides suppresses here. Uniquely among all known tragedies, however, this is the second version of the same essential myth by a single poet, as Euripides had a few years earlier staged another *Hippolytus* in which the amorous Phaedra tried openly to seduce her stepson—the kind of shocking plot Aristophanes ridiculed. While John Gibert (1997) has recently argued that we should not assume that the *Hippolytus* we have is the second version, my reading is that a movement from a more lurid plot, rejected by audience and judges, to a more "classical" version, with a first-place finish, makes more sense than the reverse.

Aphrodite would destroy the young Hippolytus because of his scorn for her and the sexuality she represents, and for his worship solely of Artemis, the virgin goddess of the hunt. The vehicle for Aphrodite's punishment is instilling desire for Hippolytus in his stepmother, Phaedra, a desire that she resists, starving herself to death, until her Nurse wheedles the truth out of her and then imparts it to Hippolytus, who angrily denounces not just Phaedra, but all women. Now incensed at him and afraid he will tell his father, Theseus, Phaedra commits suicide, but leaves a note accusing Hippolytus of rape. Theseus believes this accusation, leading him to curse his son fatally with one of the three wishes granted him by his divine father, Poseidon. After a heated dispute with Hippolytus, Theseus amends the sentence to exile. As Hippolytus leaves the city, however, a monstrous bull, sent by Poseidon in response to the curse, emerges from the sea and panics Hippolytus' horses, who drag his body all over the rocky seashore. As his mangled body is returned to his father, Artemis reveals the truth to Theseus, orders their mutual forgiveness, and establishes a cult in honor of Hippolytus.

In the City Dionysia of 428 BCE, the judges agreed that the program that included *Hippolytus* should receive the first prize. Scholars over the past century have admired the construction of this drama's plot and the complexity of its issues and characters, but they also have disagreed sharply about what the drama and its main character might have meant to its original audience. Some have seen in Hippolytus a young man whose main offense is in his very virtue, his desire to live a principled life, free from the distractions caused by the charms of Aphrodite. Others have argued that Hippolytus' aversion to sex and desire for purity are fanatical, and thus dangerous to all around him, and that his sense of innate superiority would mark him as suspicious to an audience whose ideology was fundamentally democratic. Such divisions parallel the clash in this drama between the forces of sexuality, in the form of Aphrodite, and asceticism, as represented by the virgin goddess Artemis, and this conflict is played out in the desires and actions of the characters. Phaedra's desire for her stepson Hippolytus, which she attempts to master for so long, explodes into lethal rage when he not only rejects her but also denounces her with great violence. Theseus, faced with an accusatory suicide note left by Phaedra, first fatally curses his bastard son Hippolytus, whom an Amazon queen had borne to him, and then engages in an extraordinarily aggressive argument with Hippolytus, in which the detailed accusations they fling against one another suggest a lifetime of bitterness and disappointment. This is a play about what desire, and not just carnal desire, does to people. It is also fundamentally, like *Alcestis* and *Medea,* a family tragedy; as Aristotle argued (*Poetics* 1453b15), the best tragedies are those involving actions of kin against one another.

The context of Athens in 428 BCE suggests other levels of meaning. It had been three years since the start of the Peloponnesian War, which was clearly not about to end any time soon. The war had accelerated social changes and exacerbated tensions between advocates of the new and adherents of the old that took the form of a generation gap; as Barry Strauss (1993) has argued, this generation gap is palpable in the vehemence of the argument between the father Theseus and the son Hippolytus. In 428 it had also been two years since a devastating plague had first struck Athens, the effect of which was compounded by Pericles' decision to move the populace of the surrounding countryside inside the city walls in order to keep it safe from the Spartan army. Over the course of a series of attacks from 430 to 426, the plague killed from a quarter to a third of the Athenian people. Thucydides (2.47–55) vividly depicts the suffering and social turmoil inflicted by the plague, and recent excavations in Athens have shown a profound disruption in traditional sacred burial practices during those years, as the city fell into a blind panic. The production of Euripides' *Hippolytus* fell squarely into the middle of this crisis, and, as I argue elsewhere (2007), its effects can be seen in the prominence of the language and imagery of disease to describe the suffering of Phaedra and the body of the dying Hippolytus. The sense that the gods had abandoned Athens is perhaps reflected in the indifference of Aphrodite and Artemis to the human wreckage they inflict and watch.

Pericles had died in that same plague, and Pericles had often adopted Theseus, long a central figure in Athenian self-representation, as a supreme exemplar of the mythological propaganda in the public works program on the Acropolis. Some have seen the acknowledgment of the dying Hippolytus' nobility by Theseus as an echo of Pericles' attempts to make his bastard sons legitimate citizens after the sons by his Athenian wife died during the early attack of the plague; two decades earlier, the Athenian Assembly had enacted a Periclean proposal to restrict citizenship to the sons of purely Athenian parents. The controversy over this law can be seen in a number of tragedies that involve the fate of bastard sons, including *Hippolytus*, whose title character is depicted several times lamenting his status. The contemporary cultural climate can be felt as well in Hippolytus' elitist outlook and sequestration of himself from the normal affairs of the city, both of which might have suggested the young aristocrats who were increasingly seen as a threat to the democracy of Athens.

The world of Periclean Athens is also manifest in the drama's intellectual concerns and in the language of its characters. The relationships between knowledge and action, and between nature and nurture, are particularly prominent. One of Euripides' contemporaries, Socrates, offered the paradox that humans will want to do only good provided that they know what it is, and that knowledge is therefore virtue. While it is questionable whether Euripides should be as closely associated with Socrates as Aristophanes and Nietzsche would maintain, one does see Socrates' ideas circulating through the dramas. Here, however, they seem to be evoked only to be rejected. As Phaedra contemplates her situation, she wonders about the connection between knowledge, virtue, and action: "even though / we know and understand what's right, we fail / to act accordingly" (409–11). Given the realities of human life, it is insufficient to know the good, and action will fail her. Thus Phaedra resolves to die. Yet language fails her no less than action does. The Nurse first persuasively coaxes the truth out of Phaedra, and then, after the Nurse's horror at Phaedra's quasi-incestuous desire drives her from the stage, she returns with a battery of sophistic arguments to wear down the resolve of her mistress and convince her to accept some help. Language fails Hippolytus as well, not least because the Nurse tricks him into swearing an oath of silence about his stepmother's love; faced with his father's hostility, he lapses into a formal rhetorical style that sounds as inauthentic, despite his sincerity, as Jason's before Medea.

This drama also participates in the fifth-century debate over the relative roles of nature (*physis*) and convention (*nomos*) in human excellence; today we call one aspect of this dispute "nature versus nurture." Aristocratic ideology held that excellence was inherited, passed down from father to son. This was a profoundly antidemocratic outlook, and the Sophists, who generally have taken the rap for much of what went wrong during the fifth century, should perhaps be regarded more kindly for their role in questioning the political implications of such assertions. Theseus, Hippolytus, and Phaedra all grapple with the extent to which their identities are determined by their parents. The Cretan princess Phaedra wonders why she is the third female member of her family to have fallen in love with a forbidden object: her mother, Pasiphaë, had intercourse with a bull and gave birth to the Minotaur, and her sister, Ariadne, who was abandoned by Theseus after she helped him kill the Minotaur, then loved the god Dionysus. Once Phaedra articulates this belief in the power of her heredity, she yields to the Nurse's pleas. Theseus, who has two fathers in the god Poseidon and the mortal King Aegeus of Athens, is similarly unsure about the nature and role of his parentage, since, while he quickly invokes the curses given to him by Poseidon, he then just as quickly forgets them as he exiles Hippolytus. Thus, his joy at the news of the manner of Hippolytus' death comes from the sudden reassurance that he really is the son of Poseidon. But Artemis' greeting of Theseus as "child of Aegeus" implicitly rebukes him for his all-too-human anger, as well as reminds him that Hippolytus is not the first relative he has killed, since Aegeus committed suicide when Theseus forgot to change the color of his sails from mournful black to victorious white when returning from the Minotaur quest. Hippolytus believes fervently in the power of his natural superiority and virtue, but, like so many protagonists in Greek tragedy, he is fatally wrong about his nature. To begin with, Hippolytus' inherited nature is problematic; his prayer to the statue of Artemis expresses his belief that his "wise restraint is natural / —not studied or instructed, but innate" (93–94), and he equates "wise restraint" (*sôphrosynê*) with virginity, but as the son of Theseus, a hero with multiple liaisons and wives, Hippolytus' nature would tend to the opposite direction, and thus be in conflict with the avoidance of the opposite sex that characterized his Amazon mother. Moreover, chastity in Greek culture was associated more with the nature of young women, not young men. Perhaps his virtue is more the product of his education as "the protégé of godly Pittheus" (11). But the insecurity of being the bastard son of the great hero Theseus, left in Troezen by his father who lives in Athens, with his mother mysteriously dead, creates instabilities in Hippolytus that become manifest in his language and actions. He chooses his nature, as it were, in a life separate from and utterly different from his father's; he is a uniquely male virgin, worshiping a goddess who bears a striking resemblance to his mother.

Hippolytus is destroyed for this life and for these beliefs, and he remains an anomalous character to the end of the drama. He seems reconciled to his father at the end, but some have read that reconciliation as coerced by Artemis, not as love freely given. He dies angry and resentful of the forces opposed to him. Does he understand? Has he learned? Is the cult promised by Artemis, in which young women will worship him in preparation for marriage, the kind of commemoration appropriate for this misogynistic young man? The depth of this remarkable character lies in the force of both his integrity and his failings, itself a force that has prompted such divergent critical readings from antiquity to the present.[4]

A Note about Stage Directions

Stage directions are not given in the ancient manuscripts, but here they are based on known theatrical conventions and on signals in the texts. Characters could enter the acting area from the house or from either of the two side entrances. Typically (but not always) the right entrance was used for entrances from the city, and the left from nature and the rest of the world; see Wiles (1997). For other concerns with entrances and exits (and sundry aspects of Greek theater practice), see Taplin (1978). For all stage directions in these translations, right and left refer to the audience's spatial orientation.

ROBIN MITCHELL-BOYASK

---

4. For their comments on a draft of this Introduction, I am grateful to Andromache Karanika, Laura McClure, and Laurialan Reitzammer.

Translator's Preface

Euripides wrote his plays in highly formal verse whose effects range from natural-sounding conversation in the dialogues to artfully patterned mosaics of sound, sense, and image in the choral odes. The plays are powerful in Greek because the stories are compelling, the language is beautiful, and Euripides had a brilliant eye and ear for the way people act and speak. My goal in bringing these plays into English has been to do justice to all of these elements.

The Texts

I have used as my primary text of reference J. Diggle's Oxford Classical Text (*Euripidis Fabulae*, vol. 1, 1984), and have relied heavily on the commentaries of A. M. Dale (*Alcestis*), Donald J. Mastronarde (*Medea*), Denys L. Page (*Medea*), and W. S. Barrett (*Hippolytus*), and on David Kovacs' Loeb Classical Library editions. I have also consulted D. J. Conacher's commentary on *Alcestis*, Michael R. Halleran's on *Hippolytus*, and Anthony J. Podlecki's translation of *Medea*. I was able to consult H. M. Roisman and C. A. E. Luschnig's commentary on *Alcestis* after I had finished my translation.

The line numbers in the margins are those of my English versions; the line numbers of the corresponding Greek text appear in brackets at the top of each page. In this Preface, I cite lines by their numbering in my translations.

The Language

My aim in these translations has been to be faithful to Euripides' sense and to his poetry, with all that each of these involves, including diction, tone, connotation, context, echo, image, euphony, and meter. This endeavor leads to competing claims, of course, and at different times different types of faithfulness have taken precedence over others. As much as possible (given these competing claims), I have sought to translate individual Greek words consistently: for example, *thymos* is always "spirit," and *sôphrosynê* is always "wise restraint" or a variation on that phrase. For keeping track of repetitions, Allen and Italie's *Concordance to Euripides* (1954) has been invaluable. Total consistency in this regard is neither possible nor desirable—a translation that stuck to this principle at all costs would be unreadable—but I have generally been consistent enough to enable students of the plays' language and themes to read closely with some confidence. That is, if I repeat an English word, there is a pretty good chance that it reflects a repetition in the Greek, and readers can expect that I have followed any repetitions in the Greek that are thematically significant. A detailed discussion of my practice and principles of translation (especially regarding echoes and repetitions) in the third choral ode of *Hippolytus* (1245–84) can be found in my essay "A Translator's Notebook: The Third Stasimon of Euripides' *Hippolytus*" (2007).

The Meters

Many elements of the original performances of these plays are all but lost to us: music and choreography; costumes, masks, and sets; the sound of the actors' voices. What remains in the texts is the poetry, the reason for Euripides' acclaim. These plays, like all classical Athenian tragedies, were written entirely in verse; the closest Euripides comes to prose is the occasional brief interjection, such as "Aaah!" Aside from these, every line is composed with some type of poetic rhythm. Different meters (patterns of heavy and light syllables) were traditional for different parts of each play.

In English, meter is based on patterns of stressed and unstressed syllables. Ancient Greek verse on the other hand was "quantitative," based on patterns of long and short syllables; for example, a syllable with the vowel sound "o" as in "hop" was short, and one with "o" as in "hope" was long. Despite this difference in the basis of the English and ancient Greek systems, the patterns themselves—iambic, trochaic, anapestic, dactylic—are comparable, and so it is possible to get some sense of Greek meters through their English analogues. In these translations I have used different English verse rhythms to reflect the changes in meter in the Greek originals. These meters fall into three distinct categories, each with its own texture and register: spoken dialogue, anapests (chanted or sung), and lyrics.

Spoken Dialogue

The regular meter for speech in Athenian tragedy was the iambic trimeter. An iamb, in Greek and in English, is a short syllable followed by a long syllable (or unstressed followed by stressed); for example, the word "toDAY" is an iamb. Although the Greek iambic line consists of six iambs, it is called a trimeter because it was treated as three units of two iambs each:

x-LONG-short-LONG—x-LONG-short-LONG—x-LONG-short-LONG

In the "x" (anceps) positions, a long could be substituted for a short. Aristotle said that iambic rhythm was native to everyday Greek speech, and in ordinary conversation people would unintentionally produce lines of iambic verse (*Poetics* 1449a; cf. *Rhetoric* 1408b). The same is true of contemporary English; like ancient Greek, it naturally falls into patterns of alternating light and heavy syllables. I recently received a sample packet of skin lotion with printed instructions that can pass as ordinary prose: "After cleansing and toning, smooth evenly over face. Apply to neck with gentle upward strokes." The second sentence is a perfect iambic pentameter.

The iambic pentameter is the meter I have used wherever Euripides uses iambic trimeter. As the name suggests, it is a line made of five iambs: da-DUM da-DUM da-DUM da-DUM da-DUM. Many variations are traditionally allowed, and I have treated it as essentially a line with five beats.

Anapests

I have used anapestic rhythms wherever Euripides does. An anapest is short-short-LONG, like the word "vioLIN." We tend to associate anapests with comic or children's verse:

When the Star-Belly Sneetches had frankfurter roasts . . .
(Dr. Seuss, "The Sneetches")

But anapests have been used in serious English verse as well:

For the Angel of Death spread his wings on the blast
(Lord Byron, "The Destruction of Sennacherib")

Through the gathering darkness, arise . . .
(Matthew Arnold, "Rugby Chapel: November 1857")

Anapests were used in serious contexts throughout Greek tragedy. They were often used for the exits and entrances of the chorus; they could also be used for passages in a higher emotional register than ordinary speech, or to make a transition between speaking and singing. They were either chanted ("marching anapests") or sung, with slightly different rules defining the two types. In *Medea* 104–204, Medea sings her anapests and the Nurse chants hers; I have used italics to designate the sung parts. Similarly, Euripides raises the expressive pitch when the wounded Hippolytus shifts from chanting to singing (*Hippolytus* 1537–52).

Lyric Meters

The lyric meters, which were sung, have the highest emotional coloring and stand at the greatest distance from ordinary speech. Unlike iambs and anapests, most lyric meters do not translate readily into familiar English equivalents. The most formal lyric passages are the choral odes, which were danced as well as sung. These are organized into pairs of stanzas called "strophe" and "antistrophe," occasionally followed by a third stanza with a different rhythm called an "epode." Any stanza in the text identified with one of these names was set to music and sung.

Strophes and antistrophes always match each other metrically, and the rhythmic repetition was probably emphasized by melodic phrases and dance movements that repeated or mirrored each other. This feature, called "responsion," is the one metrical attribute of Euripides' lyrics that I have consistently attempted to reproduce. For example, the first line of the strophe of the ode that begins at *Alcestis* 604, "House that always welcomes guests," is matched rhythmically by the first line of the antistrophe, "Dappled lynxes joined the throng" (611). The strophe–antistrophe structure was not limited to the chorus; it was also used in solo songs, such as the Child's song at *Alcestis* 420–43. In this song we also see that lines of iambic spoken dialogue (431–32) can intervene between the strophe and antistrophe of a lyric passage.

Dochmiacs are a type of lyric meter used to express intense excitement or agitation. They could be used in formal choral odes, for example at *Medea* 1276–1337, or in lyric dialogue, as at *Hippolytus* 901–8. In *Hippolytus* there are two songs in dochmiacs widely separated from each other but still displaying responsion: 386–402 is matched rhythmically by 734–50. There were many variations on the dochmiac, whose basic rhythm was short-LONG-short-short-LONG. As with all lyric meters, I have not tried to reproduce dochmiacs syllable for syllable, but I have tried to capture their flavor, and I have observed responsion wherever it is found in the texts.

Acknowledgments

I am delighted to thank those who helped bring this project to fruition; not least among them are the authors and editors of the commentaries and texts mentioned at the beginning of this Preface. Editor Brian Rak of Hackett Publishing Company has been extremely supportive, sage, and helpful throughout the process, and it has been a pleasure to work with Managing Editor Meera Dash. I am grateful also to the press' anonymous readers. David Kovacs read this work with great care and offered insightful suggestions, which have improved the translations in many places. I thank Robin Mitchell-Boyask for his comments on the translation, which led to further improvements, and for contributing the very useful Introduction and footnotes. My husband, John Svarlien, was always willing to lend me his ear for poetry and his good judgment when I was considering different versions of a line or passage. I am grateful to Georgetown College, especially the library, for institutional support. The University of Kentucky library, too, has been a great asset.

This volume is dedicated to my teachers at the University of Texas at Austin, the University of Virginia, and Bethesda-Chevy Chase High School, with thanks for all they have taught me about Greek and about poetry. Douglass Parker set me on the path to becoming a translator, for which I am very grateful. I count among my best experiences the time I spent studying Greek poetry with the late David Francis and Gareth Morgan, and with David Armstrong, Jenny Strauss Clay, Michael Gagarin, Thomas K. Hubbard, Richard Hunter, David Kovacs, Jon Mikalson, and Cynthia Shelmerdine.

I also thank my family, John, Aaron, and Corinna, who teach me every day about language and love.

DIANE ARNSON SVARLIEN

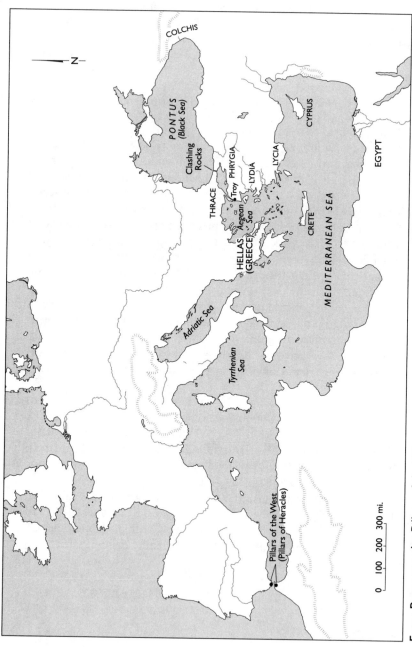

From Pontus to the Pillars of the West

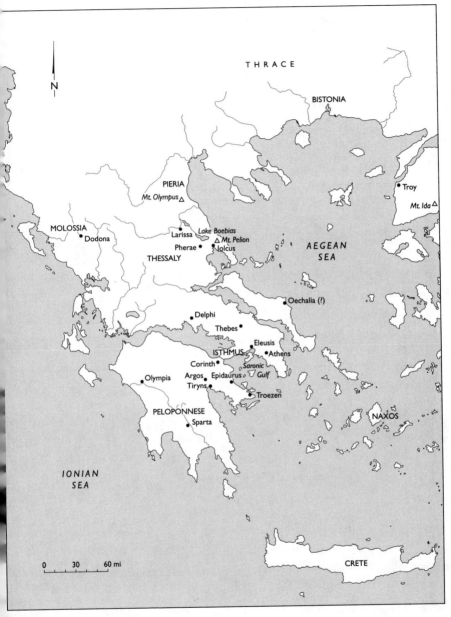

N

THRACE

BISTONIA

PIERIA

Mt. Olympus △

Troy

Mt. Ida △

MOLOSSIA

Dodona

Larissa

Lake Boebias

△ Mt. Pelion

AEGEAN
SEA

Pherae

Iolcus

THESSALY

Oechalia (?)

Delphi

Thebes

Eleusis

ISTHMUS

Athens

Corinth

Saronic
Gulf

Olympia

Argos

Epidaurus

Tiryns

Troezen

NAXOS

PELOPONNESE

Sparta

IONIAN
SEA

0   30   60 mi

CRETE

Hellas

For My Teachers

Alcestis

Alcestis: Cast of Characters

APOLLO

DEATH   (Thanatos)

CHORUS   men of Pherae

FEMALE SERVANT

ALCESTIS

ADMETUS   king of Pherae

CHILD   of Alcestis and Admetus

HERACLES

PHERES   Admetus' father

MALE SERVANT

Alcestis

SCENE: *In front of the palace of Admetus in Pherae, a town in Thessaly. Apollo, bearing his bow, emerges from the palace door.*

APOLLO:

Here is Admetus' house, where I endured
a seat of honor at the servants' table
although I am a god. Zeus was the cause:
he killed my son Asclepius[1] with a blast
of lightning to the chest. Enraged for him   5
I killed the Cyclopes, who forge the bolts
of Zeus.[2] My father paid me back for that
by forcing me to serve a mortal man.
I came to this land, tended this man's cattle,
was treated like a guest, and to this day   10
I have preserved his household. I have found
that Pheres' son is holy, like myself.
I tricked the Fates and rescued him from Hades.
The goddesses agreed to let Admetus
escape his designated day of death   15
if he could satisfy the gods below
by sending in his place another corpse.
Admetus went to everyone who loved him:
his father, and his old mother—who gave him life—
and asked them one by one if they would do it.   20
No one except his wife would die for him
and see the light no more. She's in the house now,
too weak to hold herself up, her soul subsiding.

---

1. The mythical founder of medicine is Asclepius, the son of Apollo and a mortal woman. He became so skilled at healing that he attempted to resurrect a dead man (Hippolytus) and was killed by Zeus. See the note at *Hippolytus* 1350.
2. These Cyclopes are not to be confused with the giants whose island Odysseus visits.

This is the day, you see, the fated end.

25   I'm leaving now, lest I become infected
        by death's miasma in this house I love.[3]
        Already I see Thanatos approaching:
        priest of the perished, Death himself.[4] He's here
        to take her down to the house of Hades. Now

30   his moment has come, the day he's waited for.

        (Enter Death from the right.)

DEATH:

        Hey!
        What are *you* doing here, prowling outside this house,
        Lord Phoebus Apollo? You're at it again,
        poaching, encroaching on
        honors that rightly

35   belong to the dead, to the gods down below!
        You weren't content to put off the appointed
        death of Admetus, by fooling the Fates,
        resorting to ruses![5] And now you've come after her
        fretting and meddling, armed and intrusive, for

40   Pelias' daughter,[6] who swore on her honor
        to die for her husband, let *him* off the hook.

APOLLO:

        Relax. My words are just, my actions righteous.

DEATH:

        With justice on your side, you need a weapon?

---

3. In Greek drama the gods flee at the approach of human mortality, no matter how they feel about the dying person; compare the withdrawal of Artemis as her beloved servant Hippolytus passes away (*Hippolytus* 1609–12).

4. *Thanatos* is the Greek word for death.

5. Apollo is said to have gotten the Fates drunk as part of his attempt to divert them from Admetus; see Aeschylus, *The Furies* 723–24.

6. Alcestis is the daughter of Pelias, familiar to students of Greek myth as the wicked uncle of Jason, who sent Jason on the quest for the Golden Fleece. Pelias offered Alcestis to whoever could yoke a lion and a boar together with a chariot.

APOLLO:
My custom is to have this bow with me.

DEATH:
And to help *them*, violating justice.   45

APOLLO:
I love my friend. I grieve for his disasters.

DEATH:
And so you'll rob me of this second corpse?

APOLLO:
I didn't take the first from you by force.

DEATH:
Then tell me why he's not beneath the earth.

APOLLO:
His wife stood in. The one you've come for now.   50

DEATH:
Yes. I'll drag her to the Underworld.

APOLLO:
Go on, take her. I couldn't change your mind . . .

DEATH:
From killing whom I must? I have my orders.

APOLLO:
No—only to postpone this present death.

DEATH:
Now I see the plan you're so intent on.   55

APOLLO:
Is there some way Alcestis can grow old?

DEATH:
There is no way. I, too, enjoy my honors.

APOLLO:
But what's the difference? It's one life, now or later.

DEATH:
If she dies young, my prize of honor is greater.

APOLLO:
60   The older she dies, the more lavish her funeral.

DEATH:
The rich would prosper, by your argument.

APOLLO:
Oh, you're a debater! Please—explain.

DEATH:
Those who could afford it would die old.

APOLLO:
So. You refuse to do me this one favor?

DEATH:
65   I do refuse. Remember who I am.

APOLLO:
Oh yes. Despised by gods, detested by men.

DEATH:
You can't have what isn't yours by right.

APOLLO:
You'll lose this one, for all your ruthlessness.
A man to reckon with is on his way
70   to Pheres' household, sent by Eurystheus
to fetch a chariot team from wintry Thrace.[7]

---

7. King Eurystheus of Tiryns is a cousin of the hero Heracles and the master for whom Heracles must perform his Twelve Labors. While there is no canonical version of the labors' motivation, *Alcestis* makes no reference to Heracles needing to atone for the murders of his family, so it likely engages the version that had Heracles serving Eurystheus because Zeus boasted just

Admetus' house will make this guest feel welcome,
and he'll take back Admetus' wife by force.
You'll do my will, and earn no gratitude
or favor from me. I will hate you always.   75

    (Exit Apollo to the right.)

DEATH:
  Say all you want; it won't gain you a thing.
  The woman is already on her way
  down to the house of Hades. With this sword
  I'll consecrate her to the gods below
  by shearing from her head a lock of hair.[8]   80

    *(Exit Death into the palace. The Chorus enter
    from the right and divide into two groups.)*

CHORUS:
  — Why this silence outside? Why this hush on the house?
  — There's no one around, no loved one or friend
    who could say if she's dead, if it's time for our tears
    or if Pelias' daughter still looks on the light:
    Alcestis, the queen, who the whole world agrees   85
    is a woman of greatness, the ideal wife.

            [Strophe 1]

  — Does someone hear a groan, a shout,
    Hand beating breast within the house,
    a sign that it's all over?

---

before Heracles' birth that on that day would be born a man of Zeus' line
who would rule all. Hera, in hatred of all of Zeus' bastard sons, sped up
the birth of Eurystheus, a descendant of Perseus, a son of Zeus. Heracles
thus had to serve Eurystheus (*Iliad* 19.86–105). In this labor (the eighth),
Heracles must capture the man-eating mares of King Diomedes of Thrace.

8. The ancients believed that Death or Persephone could cut off a lock of
a person's hair at the moment of death, just as a lock of hair was cut from
the head of a sacrificial victim. Mourners also cut their own hair. In
Homer's *Iliad* (23.141–42), Achilles cuts his hair, as part of his mourning
for Patroclus and preparation for his own death.

90   — No sound, and no one stationed at the gates.
              Apollo, bring us calm, come lull these waves
              O Paean, our healer.[9]

           — We would hear something, surely, if she had passed on.
           — No corpse has been carried yet out of the house.
95   — How do you know that? I'm not so sure. How can you tell?
           — How could Admetus bury his good wife
              alone, without mourners?

                          [Antistrophe 1]

           — No water here for washing hands
              (as you'd expect if she were dead),
100   no basin by the doorway.

           — No lock of hair is placed here by the door,
              no sign of mourning, not a sound of grief,
              no breast-beating women.

           — And yet this is the day—
105   — What are you saying?
           — Her appointment with death, to go under the earth.
           — You've touched a raw nerve, you've nettled my soul.
           — When good people are crushed, the decent must grieve.

              (The Chorus sing all together.)

                          [Strophe 2]

              No distant oracle
110   no ship dispatched
              to Lycia, or Ammon's desert seat[10]
              can save her poor soul now.
              The sheer drop draws near:
              the precipice, her moment of defeat.

---

9. *Paean* means "healer" and was a cult epithet of Apollo the healing god, and later of his son Asclepius, who was also the object of cult worship.

10. The Chorus in their desperation imagine traveling to the ends of the earth to find help from the gods. Apollo had an oracle in Lycia, on the south coast of modern Turkey. Zeus was also worshiped as Zeus Ammon, who had an oracle in Egypt. Apollo's primary oracle was at Delphi, Zeus' at Dodona.

What altar of the gods   115
will still receive my sacrifice, my prayer?

[Antistrophe 2]

Only Apollo's son[11]
if he were here
and looked upon the light, could save her now
from Hades' gates, the seat   120
of shadows. For he
could raise the dead—until he felt the blow
of Zeus's fiery bolt.
What hope can still deceive my pure despair?

It's all over now for the king and the queen.   125
Every god's altar is spattered with blood,
spiraling smoke. But there is no cure,
no cure at all for this evil.

(Enter a female servant from the palace door.)

But look! A servant's coming from the house
streaming in tears. What will I hear from her?   130
It's natural to grieve, if something's happened.
But I would like to learn about your mistress:
is she living still, or has she died?

SERVANT:
You might say she is both alive and dead.

CHORUS:
How could she see the light still, if she's gone?   135

SERVANT:
She's sinking, and her soul is subsiding.

CHORUS:
Poor thing! A good man, losing a fine wife.

SERVANT:
He doesn't realize it yet—he'll feel it soon.

---

11. Asclepius, as Apollo indicated earlier (4), was killed by Zeus.

CHORUS:
You're sure there really is no hope for her?

SERVANT:
140   Her fated day is here in all its force.

CHORUS:
So . . . everything she needs is being prepared?

SERVANT:
Her things are ready. Her husband will bury her.

CHORUS:
I hope she knows how glorious her death
will be, and how her greatness far surpasses
145   any woman's underneath the sun.[12]

SERVANT:
Who could possibly deny her greatness?
No word exists for one who could surpass her.
What more compelling way is there to show
how much you hold your husband first in honor
150   than to be willing to die on his behalf?
The whole town knows what she has done for him.
But listen to what she did inside the house—
you'll be astonished.
When she realized
the day had come, she bathed her pale skin
155   with water from the river. Then she took
her clothing and her lovely jewelry
from cedar chambers, and she dressed herself
as the occasion called for. At the hearth
she prayed to Hestia:[13] "Mistress, I will ask
160   one last thing. I will go beneath the earth;

---

12. Euripides uses the language of Homeric heroism to describe the actions of a woman who is in an extraordinary situation. See also the note at *Medea* 391.

13. The goddess Hestia was mistress of the hearth, the innermost part of the Greek household, and was thus particularly important to the lives of women.

I fall before you now this one last time.
Care for my motherless children. Join my son
to a loving wife, and join a noble husband
to my daughter. May they live a full
and joyful life—not like their mother,   165
dying young, destroyed before my time—
but blessed with fortune in their fatherland."

Every altar in Admetus' house
she supplicated, garlanding each one
with myrtle leaves,[14] pulling from the bough   170
each pliant, fragrant stem. Her eyes were dry;
she did not moan. Her beautiful complexion
was unchanged by the imminent disaster.

Then she came to her bedroom. There she cried,
falling onto her bed, and spoke these words: 175

"My marriage bed, O bed where I gave up
my maidenhood, my dear virginity
to him, the man for whom I now am dying:
farewell. I do not hate you, though it's you
alone who have destroyed me. It was you   180
that I would not betray, you and my husband.
I'm dying. Someone else, another woman
(whose wise restraint could not surpass my own,
but who may be, perhaps, more fortunate)
will have you."   185
                As she fell into the bed
she kissed it, and she soaked it with her tears.
Then, when those floods of tears had sated her,
she staggered up reluctantly, sinking forward,
heading for the door, but she kept turning
back to the bed, pitching back into it.   190

The children clung to their mother's clothes and sobbed.
She held them in her arms one at a time,
embraced them like a woman who is dying.
All through the house, the servants too were sobbing,

---

14. Myrtle was used in the ancient Mediterranean for ceremonial decoration and was particularly sacred to Aphrodite.

195   pitying their mistress. She extended
her hand to each of them, and spoke and listened
to every one, even the most lowly.

Such are the misfortunes of the household
of Admetus. If he had died, you know,
200   he would have left this life. But he escaped
to gain a grief he never will forget.

CHORUS:
     Admetus must be moaning bitterly
     to lose a wife as noble as Alcestis.

SERVANT:
     He's sobbing, and embracing his dear wife,
205   begging her not to betray him, wishing for
what cannot be. She's fading like an ember
growing cold, extinguished by her illness.
Exhausted, slack, a dead weight in his arms . . .[i]
Although she's barely breathing, still she longs
210   to look upon the sun's rays one last time;
for after this, she never will again.[ii]

I'll go now, and announce that you are here.
Not everybody has such kind intentions,
standing by their rulers as an ally
215   in their misfortunes. You, I know, have been
my masters' true friend for a long, long time.

(Exit Servant into the palace.)

[Strophe]

CHORUS:
     — O Zeus, how can there be
     any solution, any escape
     from the troubles our rulers face?

220   — Will someone come out? Or is it now time
     to cut my hair in grief,
     to wrap myself in mourning black?

     — It's all too clear, my friends, it's all too clear. But still

we will pray to the gods.
They have the most power.   225

— Lord Paean, Healer,[15]
devise some strategy, find some way out.

— Do something, do something! Once, in the past, you
found a way, an escape; it's time again now
to bring help, to bring some release,   230
something to counteract bloodthirsty Hades.

[Antistrophe]

— Alas . . .[iii]
You have endured a terrible shock,
son of Pheres, in losing her.

— Oh, this is too much. You'd be justified   235
in cutting your own throat
or hanging from the highest noose.

— This very day you'll see your wife, not merely loved
but the most loved of all,
descending to death.   240

(Alcestis, Admetus, and children emerge from the
palace. Alcestis, lying on a couch, is carried by
servants.)

— But look! They're coming.
She's coming from the house—her husband, too.

— Cry out and moan now, O Pherae, lamenting
for a woman of greatness fading away
like a dying coal, her disease   245
pulling her down to the caverns of Hades.

I will never say marriage
brings more joy than pain,
taking as evidence
all that I've seen before   250

---

15. *Paean* can serve as the cult title of both Apollo and his son Asclepius,
a healing deity; the word also denotes a type of song believed to have healing powers. See the note at line 92.

added to what has befallen the king:
losing his wife, a true
woman of greatness, he's
facing a life for the rest of his days
255   that is no life at all.

> *(In the following passage, Alcestis sings and
> Admetus speaks.)* [16]

ALCESTIS:

[Strophe 1]

Daylight, warmth of the sun!
And high above, vortex of racing clouds.

ADMETUS:
The sun can see our undeserved misfortune;
we're guilty of no crime against the gods.

ALCESTIS:

[Antistrophe 1]

260   *Earth, and sheltering roof!*
And dear Iolcus, fatherland, marriage bed! [17]

ADMETUS:
Raise yourself, poor thing. Please, don't betray me.
Pray to the powerful gods to have some pity.

ALCESTIS:

[Strophe 2]

I'm seeing, I'm seeing it—there is the boat
265   *in the shallows. The ferryman of corpses,*
Charon, his hand on the pole,

---

16. The contrast between the song of Alcestis and speech of Admetus is striking. The voice of Alcestis is quite emotional compared with that of her husband, whose speech seems flat. Some scholars have argued that this contrast suggests the emotional limitations of Admetus.

17. Iolcus is the home of Alcestis' father, Pelias, and of Jason as well.

calls to me now: "Why are you delaying?
Hurry! You're slowing us down!"
You see, he's rushing me, driving me on.

ADMETUS:
  Oh, god. The crossing you describe is bitter.   270
  Your fate is bleak. Our suffering is great.

ALCESTIS:

[Antistrophe 2]

He's leading, he's leading me—somebody (can't
you see?) down to the courtyard of corpses,
eyes glowing dark, his brows lowered,
glaring at me, the wingèd god Hades.[18]   275
What are you doing? Let me go!
This is the sorrowful road I must tread.

ADMETUS:
  Full of pain for those who love you. I
  will suffer most of all, along with the children.

ALCESTIS:

[Epode]

Now let me go, let me go now!   280
Lay me down, my legs have no strength.
Hades is near. My eyes fill with darkness.
Night steals over me.
Children, children, your mother no longer,
no longer exists.   285
Farewell, my children. Live joyfully
here in the daylight.

---

18. The image of Hades leading Alcestis down to the Underworld by the
wrist suggests the iconography of a wedding. Young women who died
before their weddings were said to marry death. The archetype for this is
Persephone, the bride of Hades himself. See Rehm (1994) and Foley,
"*Anodos* Dramas: Euripides' *Alcestis* and *Helen*," in Foley (2001), pp.
301–32.

ADMETUS:

    Oh, god. What you say
    is so painful to hear—
290   much worse than death, from my point of view.
    Please don't betray me, please, by the gods,
    by the motherless children you're turning your back on!
    Rise up, endure!
    With you dead, I wouldn't exist. I'd be nothing.
295   My life, or the end of it, lies in your hands.
    Yours is the love we revere, and the friendship.

ALCESTIS:

    Admetus, you can see my situation.
    Before I die, I'd like to let you know
    my wishes. I put you before myself,
300   and gave up my own life so you could live
    and look upon this daylight. I am dying,
    although I didn't have to, for your sake.
    I could have married well in Thessaly,
    had any man I wanted, lived in wealth.
305   I didn't want to live deprived of you,
    with orphaned children. Therefore I gave up
    the joys I had to live for, and my youth.
    And yet your parents both betrayed you. They
    had reached the point where death was best for them—
310   to save their child and their reputation
    would have been best. You were their only one;
    they had no hope, if *you* died, of more children.
    We could have lived our days out, you and I,
    and you would not be moaning now, bereaved,
315   caring for motherless children. As it is,
    some god arranged that things should be this way.

    Ah, well.

           You must remember what I've done,
    repay the favor. It's not possible
    to pay me back what I deserve (for nothing
320   is worth more than a life), but what I *will* ask
    is fair, as you'll agree. You love these children
    as much as I, if you have any sense.
    Let them be the masters of my home.
    Don't remarry. Spare them a stepmother,

an inferior replacement, filled with spite   325
and anger, who would raise her hand against
your children and mine.[19] I beg you, please,
don't do this, whatever else you do.
A second wife, a stepmother, is hostile
to her predecessor's children—she's a viper.   330

A male child has his father, a great tower
of strength.[iv] But you, my daughter, how will you
grow up to womanhood? What kind of wife
will your father marry after me? Let's hope
she doesn't, in the blossom of your youth,   335
cast some disgraceful slander on your name
and ruin utterly your hopes of marriage.

Your mother will never see you as a bride,
never stand beside you, give you courage
in childbirth, where a mother is most needed.   340
I have to die right now, and not tomorrow,
not the day after, but without delay
I shall be counted with those who exist no longer.
Farewell, and rejoice. My husband, you
can boast of your wife's greatness. You, my children,   345
can boast that you were born of a great woman.

CHORUS:
    Don't worry—surely I can speak for him—
    he'll do what you ask, unless his mind has gone wrong.

ADMETUS:
    So be it, have no fear. For you were mine
    in life, and when you're dead no other woman   350
    of Thessaly will ever call me husband.
    No other woman's father is so noble;
    no woman can compare with you in beauty,
    and I don't need more children. To the gods

---

19. As in *Medea* and the myths surrounding it (e.g., Ino), stepmothers are generically wicked. But is Alcestis' request that Admetus essentially live alone for the rest of his life some form of retribution for how he has handled this series of events? Note that, after this request, Alcestis' comments to her daughter (333–37) suggest that Admetus will, in fact, remarry.

355   I pray that I'll enjoy the fullest profit
from them, as I have not from you. My grief
for you will last not only for a year,
dear wife, but for as long as I shall live.
And all that time my hatred for my mother
360   and loathing for my father shall not die.
They loved me with their words, not with their actions.
But you gave the most precious thing you had
that I might live. Don't I have every reason
to moan, when I have lost a wife like you?

365   I'll put an end to all the celebrations,
garlands, drinking, revelry, and music
that filled my house before. I'll never touch
the lyre, or lift my spirits up with singing
to the Libyan flute. All my delight in life
is gone without you.
370   I'll have a sculpted image,
a likeness of your body, carved with skill,
to lay upon my bed. I'll fall upon her,
wrap my arms around her, call your name,
and think that my dear wife is in my arms,
375   though she is not. Cold comfort, I'm aware—
a frigid delight. But still, it could help ease
the heavy burden on my soul. Perhaps
you'll visit me in dreams, and bring me joy.
It's sweet to see the ones we love at night,
380   even in sleep, even very briefly.

If I had the voice of Orpheus, the power
to enchant Demeter's daughter with my song,
or words and melody that could persuade
her husband Hades, then I would have gone
385   to bring you from the Underworld.[20] The hound

---

20. The singer Orpheus lost his wife, Eurydice, to a snakebite. Overwhelmed with grief, Orpheus descended to the Underworld and asked Hades and Persephone (Demeter's daughter) for the return of Eurydice. Charmed by his songs, they agreed, on the condition that Orpheus not look back at Eurydice until he and his wife reach the surface of the earth. He cannot resist looking back, and she returns to the dead. This is not a good myth for Admetus to use here, since he, like Orpheus, fails his wife.

of Pluto[21] never could have held me back,
nor Charon, with his hand upon the oar,
conveyer of souls. I'd have brought you up
to live again in daylight.
                              Anyway,
await me there below. Prepare our home,   390
so we can be together when I die.
I'll ask to have my body laid out with yours,
side by side, in the same cedar coffin.
I hope that I may never be without you,
even in death, my only faithful friend!   395

CHORUS:
    You know that I will shoulder this grief with you,
    friend to friend. She's worthy of our sorrow.

ALCESTIS:
    Children, you have heard your father promise
    that he will never marry a new wife
    to rule you. He will not dishonor me.   400

ADMETUS:
    That's what I say. And I will keep my promise.

ALCESTIS:
    On those conditions, take these children from me.

ADMETUS:
    I do. A beloved gift from a loving hand.

ALCESTIS:
    Now you must be their mother in my place.

ADMETUS:
    I am compelled, since they're bereft of you.   405

ALCESTIS:
    Children, I'm going now. I should have lived.

---

21. Pluto is another name for Hades. His hound is the three-headed
Cerberus.

ADMETUS:
> What will I do without you, all alone?

ALCESTIS:
> Time will soften your grief. The dead are nothing.

ADMETUS:
> Please, by the gods, take me with you down below!

ALCESTIS:
410 I'm dying for you. My death is sufficient.

ADMETUS:
> Gods, what a wife you steal away from me.

ALCESTIS:
> Ah. The darkness presses on my eyes.

ADMETUS:
> My wife, if you forsake me, I'm destroyed.

ALCESTIS:
> I no longer exist. I'm nothing now.

ADMETUS:
415 Lift up your face! Please, don't desert your children.

ALCESTIS:
> Oh no, not willingly. Farewell, my dear ones.

ADMETUS:
> Look up at them, look up!

ALCESTIS:
>   I'm nothing now.

ADMETUS:
> What are you doing?

ALCESTIS:
>   Farewell.

ADMETUS:
> I am destroyed.

CHORUS:
> She's gone. Admetus' wife exists no longer.

CHILD:[22]

[Strophe]

> Oh, my lonely fate.   420
> Mother is gone—gone below.
> She exists no longer, Father,
> under the sun.
> She's left me motherless; my heart is broken.
> Look: her eyes are closed.   425
> Look: her arms are just hanging down.
> Listen, Mother, hear me, please, oh please.
> It's me, it's me, Mother—
> I'm calling you, I'm giving you a kiss.
> It's me, your little boy.   430

ADMETUS:
> She cannot hear or see you. We are stricken—
> your sister, you, and I—by grim disaster.

CHILD:

[Antistrophe]

> Father, I'm just a child:
> I'm like a ship on the waves
> all alone, without my mother,   435
> feeling so sad.
> My sister, you are suffering all this
> together with me . . .^v
> . . . Oh, Father,

---

22. Most likely, the child is a mute extra and the song is sung by the actor who plays Alcestis. The actor's mask would conceal the moving lips, and, if the child is clinging to his mother's corpse, the sound would seem to emanate from him. As earlier in his exchange with Alcestis, Admetus speaks while others sing their grief.

440   you had no profit from your marriage, none.
       You couldn't grow old with her;
       she died too soon. Mother, with you gone,
       our home is destroyed.

CHORUS:
       Admetus, you're compelled to bear up under
445   this disaster. You are not the first
       to lose a noble wife, and won't be the last.
       You realize that all of us must die.

ADMETUS:
       Yes, I know. It's not that this misfortune
       took me by surprise. I've been aware
450   that this was coming for a long time now,
       tormented by that knowledge. Now it's time
       for me to bring her body out. Stay here,
       wait for us, and sing a mournful paean,
       with no libations, to the god below.[23]

455   All those in Thessaly who are my subjects,
       express your sorrow for my wife by wearing
       black, and cutting your hair. All you who own
       a single horse, or four-horse chariot team,
       shear their manes with sharpened iron. Let there
460   be no flute sounded and no lyre plucked
       throughout the city for a full twelve months.
       For I shall never bury one more loved
       than her, nor one who treated me more kindly.
       She's worthy of my honor; she alone
465   was kind enough to die on my behalf.

       *(Exit Admetus and children into the palace with
       Alcestis' body.)*

---

23. The paean was a type of song used to signal healing, woe, and victory.
It originated as a cult song for Apollo, who also bore the cult title Paean
(see the note at line 92 above). A paean thus should not be sung to the
"god below," Hades. Any offering to a god of the earth should be accompanied by a libation of wine.

CHORUS:

[Strophe 1]

Daughter of Pelias, farewell.
May you find contentment even in Hades' dark halls,
in a home with no sunlight.
May Hades the dark-haired god be aware,
and may he whose hand is on the oar,[24]   470
the old man who steers the dead on their way,
may he realize that by far, by far
the greatest of women has been in his boat
passing through the shallows of Acheron.

[Antistrophe 1]

Poets from all around the world[25]   475
will extol your name, plucking the seven-toned lyre—
from the shell of the mountain
tortoise—and in unaccompanied hymns.
When the festive month Carneius[26] comes
and the moon in Sparta shines all night long,   480
they will sing of you—and in opulent
Athens. Your death leaves behind a rich song
for our poets to nurture and revere.

[Strophe 2]

If only I could send
you back from the chambers, the chambers of Hades   485
into the light, from the streams of Cocytus,[27]
plying the river below with my oar.
For you were his only friend:
you were the woman who loved him, and dared

---

24. Charon is the ferryman who takes the dead across the River Acheron
into the Underworld.

25. As in *Medea* (420–33), the Chorus imagine poets creating new songs
in celebration of female, not male, excellence.

26. Carneia was the Spartan festival in honor of Apollo during the month
Carneius.

27. Cocytus and Acheron (mentioned at 474) are the two rivers that
divide Hades from the land of the living.

490   to save your husband from Hades,
        giving your soul in exchange.
        May the earth lie lightly upon you, woman.
        If your husband should take a new bride
        I know that I
495   would detest him, and so will your children.

                    [Antistrophe 2]

        His mother would not defend
        her son from the grave; neither would his old father.
        . . .^{vi}
        They didn't dare rescue the child they had borne.
        They clung to their lives in the end—
500   cowards!—although they were ancient, white-haired.
        But you gave up your young life; you
        died for a man who was young.
        May it be my luck to find such a woman
        for my own loving wife—a rare prize.
505   I know that I
        would live my whole life free of sorrow.

            (Enter Heracles from the left, wearing his customary
            lion-skin and perhaps carrying his club in his hand.)

    HERACLES:
        Men of Pherae, strangers—I'm a guest here—
        tell me, will I find Admetus home?

    CHORUS:
        Heracles! Yes, Pheres' son is home.
510   But why have you come here to Thessaly?
        What obligation brings you to our city?

    HERACLES:
        A labor for Eurystheus of Tiryns.

    CHORUS:
        Where are you heading? How far must you go?

    HERACLES:
        To Thrace, to fetch the mares of Diomedes.

CHORUS:
How can you? Don't you know how he treats strangers?[28]   515

HERACLES:
I don't. I've never been to the Bistonians.[29]

CHORUS:
That team will not be yours without a battle.

HERACLES:
I have no choice. I can't refuse my labors.

CHORUS:
You know, you'll either kill or be killed there.

HERACLES:
I know. I've run this kind of race before.   520

CHORUS:
What will you gain, if you defeat their master?

HERACLES:
I'll bring the mares back to the lord of Tiryns.

CHORUS:
Those jaws will not be easy ones to bridle.

HERACLES:
Why not? Do they breathe fire from their nostrils?

CHORUS:
They tear men limb from limb with their swift jaws.   525

---

28. Thrace is typically cast as a land of savagery. Diomedes, not to be confused with the Achaean hero in Homer's *Iliad*, feeds his guests to his maneating horses, and thus is the polar opposite of Admetus as a host. Heracles is said to have later calmed the horses by feeding them Diomedes.

29. The Bistonians were a violent tribe in Thrace who, according to Apollodorus (2.5.8), sought vengeance on Heracles after he killed Diomedes and captured the horses.

HERACLES:
Wild beasts could do that; horses never could.

CHORUS:
You'll see for yourself. Their stalls are drenched with blood.

HERACLES:
The man who raised these beasts—whose son is he?

CHORUS:
Ares' son, shield-lord of golden Thrace.

HERACLES:
530   Well, that's in keeping with my destiny—
a harsh and uphill struggle, just as always:
to battle with the sons that Ares sired.
Lycaon first, then Cycnus, now the third:[30]
this contest with the master and his mares.
535   But there's no man alive who'll ever see
Alcmene's son[31] afraid of confrontation.

*(Enter Admetus from the palace. His hair has
been cut in mourning.)*

CHORUS:
Look: the ruler of this land, Admetus
himself is here; he's coming from the palace.

ADMETUS:
Greetings, son of Zeus, and Perseus'
540   great-grandson![32] I wish all the best to you.

---

30. Lycaon and Cycnus were two sons of the war god Ares, both of whom
were killed by Heracles. Lycaon's identity is obscure, but *The Shield of
Heracles,* a poem attributed to Hesiod, recounts Heracles' battle against
Ares and Cycnus.

31. Alcmene is the mortal mother of Heracles. Zeus disguised himself as
her husband, Amphitryon, in order to gain access to her bed.

32. Alcmene is descended from Perseus, whose mother, Danaë, was
impregnated by Zeus in the form of a shower of gold that fell into her lap.
Heracles is thus descended from Zeus on both sides of his family.

HERACLES:
Lord of Thessaly, all the best to you.

ADMETUS:
You're very kind. If only that could be.

HERACLES:
I see your hair has been cut. What is your grief?

ADMETUS:
This very day I have to bury someone.

HERACLES:
The gods preserve your children from all harm!   545

ADMETUS:
Not them—they're fine. My children are inside.

HERACLES:
If it's your father—well, his time had come.

ADMETUS:
He's still living, and so is my mother.

HERACLES:
Oh no. Don't tell me it's your wife, Alcestis?

ADMETUS:
There are two ways that I could speak of her.   550

HERACLES:
Well, is she dead, or is she still alive?

ADMETUS:
She exists and yet she doesn't, to my sorrow.

HERACLES:
You haven't told me anything. What is this?

ADMETUS:
Don't you know the fate she has in store?

HERACLES:

555   I know. She promised she would die for you.[33]

ADMETUS:
Under those terms, how can she still exist?

HERACLES:
Don't mourn her in advance! Wait for the day!

ADMETUS:
She's done for, really. She exists no longer.

HERACLES:
There is a difference between life and death.

ADMETUS:

560   We'll simply have to disagree on that.

HERACLES:
So—why have you been crying? Was it someone
you loved that died? A friend, a relative?

ADMETUS:
A woman. We were speaking of a woman.

HERACLES:
A relative, or from outside the family?

ADMETUS:

565   From outside, but essential to the household.

HERACLES:
How was it that she died here in your home?

---

33. Admetus has been trying to speak as evasively as possible, but he does
not seem particularly skillful at such doublespeak. Heracles, for his part,
seems unable to put the pieces together here, but it could be that the
obtuse comic Heracles is intruding on this tragic situation. Heracles was a
prominent figure in both the tragic and comic theaters, and in the latter he
is often characterized as long on muscles, short on brains.

ADMETUS:
Her father died. And then she lived with us.

HERACLES:
What bad luck.
I wish I'd come when you were not in mourning.

ADMETUS:
What do you mean? What do you have in mind?

HERACLES:
I'll find another host, another hearth.   570

ADMETUS:
No, please! My lord, don't let it come to that!

HERACLES:
To mourners, guests can only be a nuisance.

ADMETUS:
The dead are dead. Come on inside the house.

HERACLES:
Guests feasting next to mourners is disgraceful.

ADMETUS:
We'll put you in the guest quarters. They're separate.   575

HERACLES:
Please, do me a huge favor. Let me go.

ADMETUS:
No! You must not go to someone else's hearth.

        (To a servant standing by.)

You—lead this man a good distance away,
to our guest quarters. Open them, and tell
the kitchen staff to fix him a big meal.   580
And bolt the courtyard doors. It isn't right
for guests enjoying a feast to be disturbed
by moans of grief.

(Exit Heracles, led by the servant, into the palace.)

CHORUS:

> Admetus! What are you doing?
> In the face of this disaster, you would dare
585   to take a guest in? Have you lost your mind?

ADMETUS:

> What would you say if I had driven him—
> a guest who came to me—out of my house,
> out of our city? Would you have praised me then?
> Of course not. My disaster would not be
590   diminished in the least if I were rude.
> But I would be called inhospitable—
> another sorrow added to my sorrows,
> if people say my home refuses guests.
> And this guest is my greatest host, whenever
> I visit the parched land of Argos.

CHORUS:

595   Why,
> if he is such a friend, did you conceal
> the fate that has descended on you here?

ADMETUS:

> He wouldn't have been willing to come in
> if he had known about my suffering.
600   I realize not everyone would say
> I've done the right thing. Some would even claim
> I've acted senselessly. But my house doesn't
> know how to dishonor guests, or drive them out.

(Exit Admetus into the palace.)

CHORUS:

[Strophe 1]

> House that always welcomes guests,
605   house of a free and generous man,
> even Apollo, lord of the lyre, lived here,
> dared to descend, and

deigned to be a herdsman for your halls,
along the rolling slopes
piping a wedding chorus for sheep and goats.   610

[Antistrophe 1]

Dappled lynxes joined the throng
drawn by the charm of the joyful tune;
down from the mountains, banding together, came lions
burnished like copper;
spotted fawns stepped lightly to your strings   615
beneath the silver firs
filled with delight to dance to a song so rich.

[Strophe 2]

And so he makes his home and has his hearth
here in a wealth of flocks
by the glittering shallows of Lake Boebias.   620
The land that he tills, his level acreage
stretches as far as the western
stables where the horses of the sun
are kept, beyond . . . Molossia.^{vii}
His rule extends east to the sea as far as the crags   625
around Mt. Pelion.[34]

[Antistrophe 2]

And now his halls are open to receive
a guest, though his eyes are damp
and his wife, whom he loved, has just died in his house;
his grief is still recent. His nobility   630
goes to extremes to show reverence.
In good men all good qualities are found:
I truly marvel at his wisdom.

---

34. The Chorus are describing the realm of Admetus. Molossia is a western part of Thessaly. Pelion is a tall mountain in Thessaly where the centaur Chiron lives. Its trees were cut down to build the *Argo*. The Argonaut
Peleus married the nymph Thetis there, a wedding that led to both the
birth of Achilles and the Trojan War.

A man who so honors the gods is sure to do well;
635   I feel it in my soul.[35]

> (Enter Admetus from the palace, with attendants
> carrying Alcestis' body on a bier.)

ADMETUS:
Gentlemen of Pherae, my well-wishers,
her corpse has been prepared, and the attendants
have raised her up to take her to the grave.
Speak to her now, according to our custom,
640   as she goes past you on her final journey.

CHORUS:
But look, your father's coming; I recognize
his old man's gait. And he has servants with him,
carrying adornments for your wife.

> (Enter Pheres and attendants from the right side.
> The funeral procession stops and places the corpse
> of Alcestis on the ground.)

PHERES:
My child, I've come to share your sorrow. No one
645   can possibly deny that you have lost
a noble wife, a woman of restraint
and wisdom. You're compelled to bear what must
be borne, however sad and difficult.

Here: please accept these adornments. Let them go
650   below the earth with her. We have to honor
her body, since she gave her very soul
so you could live, my child. She would not
leave me childless, let me waste away
in miserable old age, deprived of you.
655   And by her noble and courageous act
she has enhanced the virtuous reputation
of all womankind.
                    Savior of my son,

---

35. The Chorus now seem convinced by Admetus' arguments and have
put aside their earlier criticism of him (583–85).

and my support when I was sinking low,
farewell! May Hades' halls be kind to you.

A marriage like that, I tell you, profits a man.   660
Otherwise, why bother getting married?

ADMETUS:
You weren't invited to this funeral
by me, and I do not consider you
a well-wisher, much less a loved one. She
will not be dressed in your adornments, never.   665
She'll be buried with no help from you.
The time to share my pain was then, when I
was facing death. But you stood back, old man,
and let somebody else die, someone young!
And now you'll mourn her? I just can't believe   670
you really are my father, or that she
who claims to be my mother really bore me.
I must have been the child of some slave
and someone slipped me under your wife's breast!

Under pressure, you showed what you were made of;   675
I don't consider myself your son. But—hey!
You win first prize for cowardice:
a man like you, who'd reached the end of life,
unwilling—just not brave enough—to die
for his own son. Instead, you let a woman   680
—a woman from outside the family—perish.
She's the one, the only one, that I
regard as my true mother and my father.[36]
That's nothing more than simple justice.
                                                Yet
you could have come across with flying colors: 685
dying for your child, when you had
so little time remaining anyway.[viii]
And really, you've had everything a man
could be considered fortunate for having.
When you were young, you were the king, and then   690

---

36. Admetus here perhaps echoes the words of Andromache to Hector,
that he is her father and mother (and brother), because her entire birth
family is dead (*Iliad* 6.429–30).

you had me—a son who could inherit
your whole estate. You didn't have to worry
that you'd die childless, and leave your home
without an heir, for strangers to pick over.

695 You cannot claim that I've dishonored you
in your old age, and that's why you betrayed me
and left me to die. I have been completely
reverent toward you—and this is how
you and my mother have repaid the favor.

700 You'd better hurry up and have more children
to tend to your old age, and when you die
to wrap you in your shroud and lay you out.
I'll never bury you with my own hand.
I might as well be dead, for all the help

705 I got from you. If I still see the light—
if someone else has saved me—*she's* the one
whose child I am, whose old age I should nurture.

Old men pray for death, but what's the point?
They grumble about aging, but when the end

710 approaches, suddenly they want to live
and old age doesn't seem so bad to them.

CHORUS:
Stop it! This disaster is enough.
Don't make your father any angrier.

PHERES:
Child, who do you think I am? Some Lydian

715 or Phrygian slave[37] you bought and paid for? Listen,
don't speak to me that way. I'm a Thessalian—
freeborn, legitimate—so was my father.
This is an outrage! Where do you get off
flinging these childish accusations at me?

720 I gave you life, and raised you to be master
of this estate; I'm not obliged to die
to suit your whims. There's no ancestral custom

---

37. Lydia and Phrygia were territories in Asia Minor (modern Turkey)
and a common source of slaves in Euripides' time. The purchase of such
slaves would have been an anachronism for the heroic period.

that fathers give their lives to save their children—
no Greek law, either. Your fortune, good or bad,
is yours, and no one else's. What I owe you   725
you have already: you rule a wide domain,
and I will leave you many acres more,
as my father did for me. So tell me this:
how have I wronged you? How have you been deprived?
Don't die for me, and I won't die for you.   730
You love to be alive, to see the daylight:
what makes you think your father doesn't? Really,
the way I see it, we'll have lots of time
once we go down below. Our lives are short;
still, they're sweet. So, you put up a fight,   735
got out of dying, shamelessly stayed alive,
avoided your due fate by killing her.
You're calling *me* a coward? You're the worst!
You've been outdone by your wife, who had the courage
to give her own life for her fine young man.   740
You've found a smart alternative to death:
just persuade your current wife to die
on your behalf! And then you blame your loved ones
if they won't do it, coward that you are!
Give me a break. You love your life, of course,   745
but so does everyone. If you go on
insulting me, then be prepared to hear
some really ugly truths about yourself.

CHORUS:
    This is dreadful. You both have said too much.
    Sir, stop speaking ill of your own son.   750

ADMETUS:
    Go ahead and speak. I've spoken *my* mind.
    The truth may hurt, but you should not have wronged me.

PHERES:
    It would have been more wrong to die for you!

ADMETUS:
    Is dying old the same as dying young?

PHERES:

755   We only have one life to live. Not two.

ADMETUS:

Then may you live a longer life than Zeus!

PHERES:

You'd curse your parents? What harm have you suffered?

ADMETUS:

I see that you're in love with a long life.

PHERES:

And you? This corpse here—shouldn't it be yours?

ADMETUS:

760   This corpse is proof of your own cowardice.

PHERES:

You can't claim that she died because of us.

ADMETUS:

My god.
I hope that you'll need *me* one day. Just wait.

PHERES:

Go find more wives, so more women can die!

ADMETUS:

You weren't willing to die. You should be ashamed.

PHERES:

765   I love this god-given daylight, son. I love it.

ADMETUS:

You're not a man. You lack the temperament.

PHERES:

Well, you're not gloating over my old corpse.

ADMETUS:

At least you'll be disgraced when you do die.

PHERES:
Who cares what people say then? I'll be dead.

ADMETUS:
My god, old age is shameless. It's too much.   770

PHERES:
She wasn't shameless. She was just a moron.

ADMETUS:
Get out of my sight! Let me bury her.

PHERES:
I'm leaving. Go ahead and bury her,
since you're her murderer. You're going to owe
the blood-price to her relatives. Acastus   775
will avenge his sister, if he's still a man.[38]

ADMETUS:
Go to hell, you and the woman you live with.
Grow old childless, just as you deserve,
although your son's alive. Never, never again
will you and I live under the same roof.   780
If I could have had heralds to proclaim
my full rejection of my father's hearth,
I would have done it.

        (*Exit Pheres to the right. Admetus turns to his
        attendants and the Chorus.*)

                        As for us, we must
bear the grief at hand. It's time to go,
to give her corpse its final obsequies.   785

CHORUS:
Alas, alas, for your unflinching nerve!

---

38. Acastus, brother of Alcestis and son of Pelias, takes over the kingdom
of Iolcus from Jason after Medea has arranged for the daughters of Pelias
to kill their father in the belief that they are restoring his youth (Apollodorus 1.9.27). See the note at *Medea* 13.

Noble Alcestis, greatest of women,
farewell. May the gods of the Underworld, Hermes[39]
and Hades, receive you with kindness. If any
790   advantage exists there for those who are good,
may you have it, when you are the honored attendant
of Hades' young bride.

    *(Exit Admetus, the Chorus, and attendants with
the body of Alcestis to the right.)*[40]

    (Enter a male servant from the palace.)

SERVANT:
The guests I've seen here in Admetus' house
have been from everywhere, and I've served hundreds.
795   But never have I welcomed to this hearth
a guest more rude, more utterly offensive
than this one.

        First of all, he had the nerve
to come inside, although he clearly saw
my master was in mourning. Once he's in
800   he lacks the simple wisdom and restraint
to take the hospitality that's offered—
he's aware of this disaster, knows what's happened!
Still, whatever we don't bring, he asks for.
He takes an ivy goblet in his hands
805   and drinks the black grape's undiluted offspring
until the fire of wine has warmed his mind.[41]
He garlands his head with pliant myrtle stems[42]
and bellows tunelessly. A double melody

---

39. One of Hermes' functions is to take the souls of the dead to Hades.

40. The departure of the Chorus from the orchestra before the end of the drama is extremely rare, occurring otherwise only in *The Furies* of Aeschylus, Sophocles' *Ajax,* and Euripides' *Helen.* Their exit marks an important shift in the drama's action.

41. Heracles is particularly characterized by gluttony, and his excessive consumption of wine, food, and women is frequently a source of humor in comedy and the cause of disaster in tragedy.

42. Myrtle had been used by Alcestis in her ritual preparations for death (169–71). Its reappearance here suggests that Heracles has picked up stems from her supply.

was heard then: he was belting out his song,
with no respect for the sorrows of the household, 810
while we, the servants, wailed for our mistress.
And yet we hid our weeping from the guest,
just as Admetus ordered. So here I am now
regaling in our halls this guest, this lout,
this thug, while *she's* been carried from the house 815
and I couldn't follow after her, extend
my hand, as I shed tears for my own mistress.
She was a mother to me, to all the servants—
always getting us out of trouble, always
calming down her husband. It's only natural 820
that I should hate this guest for showing up
at a time like this.

> (Enter Heracles, drunk, from the palace.)

HERACLES:
              You there, so high and mighty,
all wrapped up in your worries! Servants shouldn't
be grim with guests. They should be welcoming
and friendly. Here I am, your master's own 825
companion, and you greet me with a hateful
scowl and knitted brows, although this grief
is over an outsider. Come here—let me
tell you something that will make you wiser.
Do you know what human life is all about? 830
I think you don't. How could you? Listen to me:
We all must die. That goes for me and you,
and no man living has the slightest clue
if he'll live another day. Out of the blue
comes all our fortune. Scientists pursue 835
the truth, and teachers teach their arts and skills,
but still we know less than we ever knew.
You've heard what I have to say. Now, have a drink!
Enjoy yourself! The life you live today
is yours, and all the rest belongs to fortune. 840
Honor the god who is by far the sweetest
to mortals: honor kindly Aphrodite.
As for all the rest, forget it. Listen
to what I say, if you think it makes sense.

845 I think it does. Why not forget your pain
and drink with me? Fling your cares aside,
put garlands on your head!^{ix} I have no doubt
that volleys of drink will help unmoor your mind
and free it from its grim, compacted state.
850 We're mortal. We must keep our thoughts in line.
Those high and mighty types with knitted brows,
as far as I can judge, aren't living life
at all; they're just enduring a disaster.

SERVANT:
I know all that. But now is not the time
855 for reveling and laughter. Not for us.

HERACLES:
A woman died, but she was unrelated.
Don't get upset. Your masters are still living.

SERVANT:
Still living? Don't you know what's happened here?

HERACLES:
I do, unless your master lied to me.

SERVANT:
860 That man is too hospitable by far.

HERACLES:
If an outsider dies, should I be slighted?

SERVANT:
But she was all too much an insider.

HERACLES:
There's some disaster here he hasn't told me.

SERVANT:
Farewell. Leave us to mourn our masters' troubles.

HERACLES:
865 This doesn't sound like grief outside the family.

SERVANT:
If it were, I wouldn't mind your reveling.

HERACLES:
Has my host done a dreadful wrong to me?

SERVANT:
You came at a bad time for visitors.ˣ
Dear guest, it was Admetus' wife who died.

HERACLES:
What are you saying? And you still entertained me? 870

SERVANT:
He was ashamed to drive you from the house.

HERACLES:
Poor man. What a companion you have lost.

SERVANT:
She's not the only one destroyed. We all are.

HERACLES:
I did notice—I saw—his eyes were wet!
His shorn hair, his expression! But he insisted 875
that it was an outsider's funeral.
I knew I shouldn't fling the doors open wide,
shouldn't drink in the home of a generous host
when that was happening. Yet here I am
with garlands on my head!
                              And you! You didn't 880
tell me just how much this household suffered.
Where is he burying her? Where can I find her?

SERVANT:
Along the road that leads straight to Larissa,[43]
you'll see her stone tomb, just outside the city.

(Exit Servant into the palace.)

---

43. A town in Thessaly.

HERACLES:

885
Now, my bold hand and enduring heart,
it's time to show what kind of son Alcmene,
daughter of Electryon of Tiryns,
bore to father Zeus. I must repay
the favor to Admetus; I will save

890
his wife who died, Alcestis, and restore her
to this house. I'll stalk the lord of corpses,
black-winged Death; I think that I will find him
slurping blood from offerings near the tomb.
If I can rush out from my hiding-place

895
and get my arms around him, squeeze his ribs,
then no one on this earth can rescue him
until he gives that woman back. But if
I miss my prey, if he won't come to drink
the clotted blood, then I will go below

900
to the sunless home of Korê and her lord.[44]
I'll ask them for Alcestis, and I think
that I will bring her back, deliver her
back into the hands of my dear host
who didn't drive me off, but took me in

905
although his house was stricken by a grim
disaster. He was noble, he revered me,
and hid his troubles. Is there any man
in all of Thessaly, in all of Greece,
who's more hospitable? This noble man

910
will never say the man he helped was worthless.

*(Exit Heracles to the right. Enter Admetus, Chorus,
and funeral procession from the right.)*[45]

ADMETUS:
Oh,
hateful approach, how I hate to lay eyes

---

44. *Korê*, "the girl," is a cult title for Persephone, daughter of Demeter, taken by Hades to the Underworld to be his bride.

45. Since Heracles goes to, and the others come from, the same place, there must be a slight pause in the action here in order that they not be seen passing each other. The return of the Chorus marks the completion of the turn of the plot's trajectory.

on a house that is vacant.
Oh, poor me.   *(Groans.)*

Where can I even stand? Can I walk? Can I speak?
Can I leave words unsaid? I wish I could die.   915
My mother bore me to a burdensome fate.
I envy the dead; I'm in love with their peace;
I wish I could dwell in their halls. There's no joy
for me anymore in the rays of the sun,
nor in setting my foot on the earth, now that Death   920
has snatched her away as a hostage to Hades.

CHORUS:

[Strophe 1]

Go in, go in: enter the inner rooms.

ADMETUS: *(Groans.)*

CHORUS:
The things you've suffered justify your groans.

ADMETUS:
Oh, god.

CHORUS:
I know the misery you've endured.

ADMETUS:
Oh no.

CHORUS:
You're not helping the one who has died.   925

ADMETUS:
Poor me.

CHORUS:
It's painful to never again
see the face of the wife you love dearly.

ADMETUS:
   You've reminded me of the wound to my heart.
   What more terrible thing can a man undergo
930   than to lose a true wife? If only we'd never
   married and lived in this house. How I envy
   those who stay single, who never have children,
   have only one life to be worried about—
   a bearable burden.
935   But who can endure seeing children get ill
   or wives carried out of their bedrooms by death?
   It's simpler by far to stay single and childless
   all through your life.

CHORUS:

[Antistrophe 1]

   Begin, begin, to wrestle with your grief.

ADMETUS: *(Groans.)*

CHORUS:
940   You set no limit on your suffering.

ADMETUS:
   Oh, god.

CHORUS:
      It's difficult to endure. Yet still . . .

ADMETUS:
   Oh no.

CHORUS:
      Be strong. You are not the first one—

ADMETUS:
   Poor me.

CHORUS:
      —whose wife has died young. Everyone
   who is mortal endures some disaster.

ADMETUS:
Oh pain that stretches endlessly, oh sorrow   945
for loved ones beneath the earth.
Why did you stop me from hurling my body
into the hollow recess of her grave
to lie there with her, with the greatest of women?
Hades would have our two lives, our two souls—   950
true to each other as we crossed the shallows
together, below the earth's surface.

CHORUS:

[Strophe 2]

In my own family
was a man who lost his son, his only child.
He had reason for sadness. And yet   955
He took it well enough, though his son was gone,
and his years were slipping away;
already his hair was gray.

ADMETUS:
My home, my own shelter! But how can I enter,
how can I live there? My fate is so changed,   960
I've fallen so far. Oh, god. I remember
bringing my bride here, holding her hand
while Pelian pine torches blazed all around us.
A great crowd of revelers sang out the wedding-hymn,
calling us lucky, me and my wife—   965
my wife who is dead now! We both came from noble
families, aristocrats. Perfectly matched!
Now for my hymn I have moans of lament;
instead of white robes, the black garments of grief
accompany me to my house, and inside   970
to the empty bed that awaits me.

CHORUS:

[Antistrophe 2]

When you were happy
you were struck by pain that found you unprepared.
But you're safe, you're alive. Your wife died

975 and left behind her love. Is her death unique?
Many wives in years that have passed
already have met their deaths.

ADMETUS:
Friends, it may not seem this way to you—
still, I think my wife's fate, compared to mine,
980 is happier. No pain will ever touch her;
her reputation shines; she's through at last
with all her toil. But I, who dodged my fate,
who wasn't supposed to live, will spend my years
in sorrow—I have just now realized.[46]
985 How can I stand to go inside this house?
Whom can I speak to, whom can I listen to
with any pleasure there inside? And where
am I supposed to turn? If I go in,
the house's loneliness will drive me out
990 when I see my wife's bed empty, and the chairs
she used to sit in, and the unwashed floors
all through the house—our children all in tears
and clinging to my knees, our servants moaning
because the house has lost so great a mistress.
995 That's what it will be like inside. And outside:
wedding celebrations, gatherings
in Thessaly, crowded with young women,
will be unbearable. I won't be able
to look at women my wife's age. It's just
1000 too difficult. And anyone who's hostile
to me in any way will say, "Look there:
that man should be ashamed that he's alive.
He didn't dare to die! He sent his wife
to take his place, and coward that he is,
1005 escaped from Hades! Can he even claim
to be a man? He hates his parents, yet
he himself was unwilling to die."
This is the type of slander I'll endure,

---

46. Late learning is a common trope in Greek tragedy. Usually characters realize the truth just as or after their actions lead to their downfall. Here, however, Admetus fully understands the effects of his evasion of death just as Heracles returns to reverse them.

on top of all my troubles. Tell me, friends:
how am I better off now, being alive,   1010
with all this pain and all this ugly talk?

CHORUS:

[Strophe 1]

I've flown up to the heavens;
I've studied every art the Muses teach;
I've tested every argument and found
there is no power stronger   1015
than Compulsion;
there's no drug, no
incantation
in the tablets
of the Thracians   1020
that record the voice of Orpheus.
Even the drugs that Phoebus Apollo
gave to Asclepius' sons—
herbs that help suffering mortals—
can't compare with her power.   1025

[Antistrophe 1]

Compulsion! She alone has
no altar to approach; no sacrifice
can turn her head; no image shows her form.
I pray you, don't oppress me:
Holy one, stay   1030
at a distance.
Even Zeus must
work beside you
when he brings his
will to pass, and nods his mighty head.   1035
Even the iron of the Chalybes' forge[47]
you can subdue with your strength;
your sheer, intractable spirit
knows no reverence at all.

---

47. The Chalybes, or Chalybi, a tribe living on the Black Sea, were
renowned for their skill at forging iron.

(The Chorus turn to Admetus.)

[Strophe 2]

1040   You're caught in the goddess' inescapable bonds.
        Be brave, for your tears will never restore
        those who have died and gone down below.
        Even the gods' own children
        fade into the darkness of death.
1045   She was loved when she was among us;
        in death she will be loved.
        The wife you brought to your bed
        was the most noble of all.

[Antistrophe 2]

        Don't let your wife's tomb be considered a place of death;
1050   let her, like a god, be honored by all:
        travelers who pass on this rolling slope
        seeing her grave, will call out,
        "That one, long ago, gave her life
        for her husband; now she is blessèd.
1055   Holy one, hail! Be kind.
        Grant to me all I desire."
        This is the fame she will have.

        *(Enter Heracles from the right with Alcestis. She is
        unrecognizable to Admetus, veiled in the manner
        of a bride.)*

        Admetus, look: the child of Alcmene
        is coming this way, to your hearth, it seems.[48]

---

48. This last part of the drama, the exodus, is a recognition scene, a type
frequently deployed with great skill by Euripides to both comic effect
(for example, here and in *Iphigenia among the Taurians* when Iphigenia
and Orestes rediscover each other) and tragic (for example, in the *Bacchae* when Agavê awakes and realizes that she holds her son's severed
head in her hands). In *Poetics* 1452a30, Aristotle argues that in the best
tragedies recognition and the reversal of the plot's direction occur at the
same time.

HERACLES:
    A man should feel free to speak his mind,   1060
    Admetus, when he's speaking to a friend.
    It isn't right to store up blame in silence,
    keeping it inside. When you had troubles
    I should have stood beside you as a friend.
    But you refused to say it was your wife   1065
    whose body was laid out. You took me in,
    made me a guest in your house, as if your grief
    was over an outsider. I put on
    garlands, poured libations to the gods,
    right there in your house, with all its sorrow.   1070
    I blame you—really—for what you did to me.
    But I don't want to hurt you when you're down.
    I'll tell you why I've come back here. This woman—
    take her, keep her safe for me until
    I kill the king of the Bistonians   1075
    and bring the Thracian mares back here with me.
    But if—and how I hope that this won't happen!—
    I don't come back, then I give her to you
    to be a servant in your house. She cost me
    a lot of toil. I came across a contest,   1080
    a public opportunity for athletes—
    a worthy challenge, and I won. This woman
    was my victory prize.[49] The lighter events
    awarded horses to the winners. Boxing
    and wrestling, the greater competitions,   1085
    awarded cattle, and a woman, too.
    Since I was right there, it would have been a shame
    to miss this chance to build my reputation
    and win some profit. Anyway, this woman
    is yours to care for, as I said. I haven't   1090
    stolen her; I won her with my labor.
    Perhaps in time you'll praise me for this, too.

ADMETUS:
    I meant no disrespect, and absolutely

---

49. The winning of a woman in an athletic contest was a common motif
in Indo-European myth; for example, Draupadi by Arjuna in the Sanskrit
Mahabharata, and Penelope (twice!) by Odysseus in the *Odyssey*.

did not consider you an enemy
1095   when I concealed my poor wife's sad misfortune.
It would have been pain laid on top of pain
if you had moved on to some other host.
It was enough for me to mourn my loss.
As for this woman, please, my lord, I beg you,
1100   if it's possible, command some other
Thessalian to keep her, someone else
who hasn't suffered as I have. You know many
willing hosts in Pherae. Don't remind me
of all my sorrow. Seeing her in the house
1105   I could never hold back my tears. Please don't
afflict me; I already am afflicted.
I already grieve enough for my disasters.
And where would she be taken care of here
in my house, this young woman? I can tell
1110   she's young, to judge from clothing and adornments.[50]
Is she supposed to share the house with men?
Among young males, how will she stay pure?
Heracles, a young man in his prime
is not easy to restrain. I'm looking out
1115   for you and what is yours. Or should I just
take care of her in my dead wife's own bedroom?
How can I let another in *her* bed?
I fear I'd be reproached: first, by the people,
who'd say that I'd betrayed my rescuer
1120   and fallen into bed with another young woman—
and then, I really must respect the dead;
I have to think of her.
                              Whoever you are,
woman, you resemble my Alcestis
in shape. Your body is like hers. Oh, god.
1125   Please—take this woman away where I can't see her.
By all the gods, stop tightening the grip

---

50. Much was made earlier (155–58) of the special clothing Alcestis had
put on for her death. There is no reason to believe that she would change
attire during or after her rescue by Heracles; so why does Admetus not
recognize what she was wearing when she died? On these and other matters, the discussion by Roisman and Luschnig (2003), pp. 208–11, is
thought-provoking.

that holds me fast already. When I look
at her, I think I see my wife. My heart
is pounding, tears are bursting from my eyes.
I'm suffering. Oh, I have just now tasted   1130
the real bitterness of all my pain.

CHORUS:
  I wouldn't say that things had worked out well.
  But whatever the gods send has to be endured.

HERACLES:
  If only I had strength enough to bring
  your wife back from the halls below to daylight.   1135
  If only I could do that favor for you.

ADMETUS:
  I know that you would like to. But what's the point?
  The dead cannot be brought back to the light.

HERACLES:
  Don't overdo your grief. Be moderate.

ADMETUS:
  It's easy to give advice. It's hard to suffer.   1140

HERACLES:
  What good would it do to mourn for her forever?

ADMETUS:
  I know, I know. But some desire compels me.

HERACLES:
  You love the one who died. That's cause for tears.

ADMETUS:
  She has destroyed me, more than I can say.

HERACLES:
  You've lost a noble wife. Who could deny it?   1145

ADMETUS:
  This man will never again enjoy his life.

HERACLES:
Your grief is at its height. Time will soften it.

ADMETUS:
Yes, if what you mean by "time" is death.

HERACLES:
A woman—a new marriage—will help heal you.

ADMETUS:
1150   Don't say that! How could you? I'm appalled.

HERACLES:
What? You won't marry? You'll keep a widower's bed?

ADMETUS:
The woman does not exist who will lie beside me.

HERACLES:
You don't suppose you're helping the one who died?

ADMETUS:
She must be honored, wherever she may be.

HERACLES:
1155   I praise you—really—but you're still a fool.

ADMETUS:
Call me anything—except a bridegroom.

HERACLES:
I admire your fidelity to your wife.

ADMETUS:
Although she's gone, I'd rather die than betray her.

HERACLES:
Be noble—take this woman into the house.

ADMETUS:
1160   No! I beg you by your father Zeus.

HERACLES:
If you don't do this, you'll be doing wrong.

ADMETUS:
But if I do, the pain will pierce my heart.

HERACLES:
Trust me. This favor may be what you need.

ADMETUS:
My god.
I wish you'd never won her in that contest.

HERACLES:
You share my victory when I'm the victor.   1165

ADMETUS:
A lovely thought. But let that woman leave.

HERACLES:
If she has to, fine. But does she have to?

ADMETUS:
She has to. If you won't be angry with me.

HERACLES:
I know something that makes me so intent on this.

ADMETUS:
You win, then. But I have to say I am not pleased.   1170

HERACLES:
A time will come when you will praise me. Trust me.

ADMETUS: (To his servants.)
Bring her in, if she has to go inside.

HERACLES:
I'd rather not let servants take this woman.

ADMETUS:
All right—you take her in the house yourself, then.

HERACLES:
1175   I must deliver her to your own hands.

ADMETUS:
I won't touch her. But she may go in the house.

HERACLES:
I trust in your right hand alone, no other's.

ADMETUS:
My lord, you're forcing me against my will.

HERACLES:
Be brave. Reach out your hand and touch this guest.[51]

ADMETUS:
1180   I'm reaching out—as if to behead a Gorgon.[52]

(Admetus reaches out to Alcestis, his face averted.)

HERACLES:
Do you have her?

ADMETUS:
             Yes, I do.

HERACLES:
                 Take care of her;
one day you'll declare the son of Zeus
is a noble guest. Look at her! Does she resemble
your wife? Forget your pain; enjoy your fortune!

---

51. Heracles transforms the dynamics of the guest-host relationship. Admetus must now treat his wife with the same honor with which he has treated guests such as Heracles.

52. The hero Perseus, grandfather of Heracles, beheaded the Gorgon Medusa. Because Medusa could petrify her attackers by sight, Perseus could attack her only by not looking directly at her.

(As Heracles speaks these lines he unveils Alcestis.
Admetus sees and recognizes Alcestis' face.)[53]

ADMETUS:
Oh, gods, what shall I say? I never hoped   1185
for such a miracle. I'm stunned. Is she my wife,
or has some god deceived my mind with joy?

HERACLES:
There's no deception. You're looking at your wife.

ADMETUS:
But what if she's an Underworld ghost?

HERACLES:
Your guest is no conveyer of dead souls.   1190

ADMETUS:
Is it really her? The one I buried? My wife?

HERACLES:
Yes—
I'm not surprised you can't believe your fortune.

ADMETUS:
Can I touch her? Speak to her? My wife's alive?

HERACLES:
Speak to her. You have all you desire.

ADMETUS:
Oh, most beloved face, beloved body!   1195
Beyond all hope, I see you, I have my wife!

HERACLES:
She's yours. I pray the gods will feel no envy.

---

53. The unveiling suggests a wedding ceremony. Greek culture frequently
conflated wedding and funeral imagery. On such matters in *Alcestis*, see
Rehm (1994), pp. 84–96.

ADMETUS:
O highborn child of almighty Zeus,
good luck to you, and may your father take
1200 good care of you, for you alone have saved me.
How did you bring her back into the light?

HERACLES:
I fought the god who held her in his power.

ADMETUS:
Where did it take place, this contest with Death?

HERACLES:
Right by the tomb. I rushed at him and grabbed him.

ADMETUS:
1205 And why is she just standing there in silence?

HERACLES:
It's not yet right for you to hear her voice;
she's consecrated to the gods below
and will not be released until the third
day's light has come. Go on, take her inside.
1210 Admetus, please continue ever after
to be a just man, pious toward your guests.
And now, farewell. I must complete the labor
laid out for me by Sthenelus' tyrant son.[54]

ADMETUS:
Please stay awhile and share our hearth with us.

HERACLES:
1215 Some other time. But I must hurry now.

(Heracles exits to the left.)

ADMETUS:
Good fortune to you, and a speedy journey home.

---

54. Eurystheus; see the note at line 71. Sthenelus was a son of Perseus and Andromeda who married a daughter of Pelops and ruled Mycenae.

To all the citizens and all the kingdom
I say: let there be dancing now, and singing;
let fragrant smoke rise up from every altar
in honor of this splendid outcome. Now   1220
my life has been transformed—much for the better.
I can't deny that I'm a lucky man!

(Admetus and Alcestis enter the palace.)

CHORUS:
The designs of the deities take many forms;
they often accomplish what no one would hope for.
What we expect may not happen at all,   1225
while the gods find a way, against all expectation,
to do what they want, however surprising.
And that is exactly how this case turned out.[xi]

Medea

Medea: Cast of Characters

NURSE	of Medea
TUTOR	of Medea and Jason's children
MEDEA	
CHORUS	women of Corinth
CREON	king of Corinth
JASON	
AEGEUS	king of Athens
MESSENGER	
CHILDREN	of Medea and Jason

Medea

SCENE: *A normal house on a street in Corinth. The*
            elderly Nurse steps out of its front door.

NURSE:

    I wish the *Argo* never had set sail,
    had never flown to Colchis through the dark
    Clashing Rocks;[1] I wish the pines had never
    been felled along the hollows on the slopes
    of Pelion,[2] to fit their hands with oars—   5
    those heroes who went off to seek the golden
    pelt for Pelias. My mistress then,
    Medea, never would have sailed away
    to reach the towers of Iolcus' land;[3]
    the sight of Jason never would have stunned   10
    her spirit with desire. She would have never
    persuaded Pelias' daughters to kill their father,
    never had to come to this land—Corinth.[4]

---

1. The *Argo* was the ship Jason had constructed with the help of Athena
for his voyage to the Black Sea in order to obtain the Golden Fleece, which
he needed to regain his place as rightful heir to the throne of Iolcus. King
Pelias, who had seized the throne from Jason's father, sent him on this
quest in order to rid himself of Jason when the latter returned from exile.
To reach Colchis, a kingdom on the shore of the Black Sea, the *Argo* had
to sail through the Clashing Rocks, located near the mouth of the
Bosporus. Colchis was the home of Medea.
2. Pelion is a tall mountain in Thessaly, home of the centaur Chiron who
raised Jason during his exile as a baby and youth.
3. Iolcus is a town on the southern coast of Thessaly. Its modern name is
Volo.
4. After Jason returned with the Golden Fleece, Pelias still refused to give
up the throne, so Medea demonstrated to his daughters a spell for restoring their father's youth: she took an old ram, dismembered it, and cooked
its parts in a pot. Out jumped a young ram. Their attempt to perform the
same trick with their father resulted in his death. Euripides' debut in 455
was with a play based on this legend. Jason and Medea then went into exile,

Here she's lived in exile with her husband
15 and children, and Medea's presence pleased
the citizens. For her part, she complied
with Jason in all things. There is no greater
security than this in all the world:
when a wife does not oppose her husband.
20 But now, there's only hatred. What should be
most loved has been contaminated, stricken
since Jason has betrayed them—his own children,
and my lady, for a royal bed.
He's married into power: Creon's daughter.[5]
25 Poor Medea, mournful and dishonored,
shrieks at his broken oaths, the promise sealed
with his right hand (the greatest pledge there is)—
she calls the gods to witness just how well
Jason has repaid her. She won't touch food;
30 surrendering to pain, she melts away
her days in tears, ever since she learned
of this injustice. She won't raise her face;
her eyes are glued to the ground. Friends talk to her,
try to give her good advice; she listens
35 the way a rock does, or an ocean wave.
At most, she'll turn her pale neck aside,
sobbing to herself for her dear father,
her land, her home, and all that she betrayed
for Jason, who now holds her in dishonor.
40 This disaster made her realize:
a fatherland is no small thing to lose.
She hates her children, feels no joy in seeing them.
I'm afraid she might be plotting something.[6]

---

eventually reaching Corinth, a prominent city in the northern Peloponnese near the Isthmus. During the year before the production of Euripides' *Medea*, tensions ran high between Athens and Corinth, which then fought against Athens during the Peloponnesian War.

5. This Creon should not be confused with the character in the Oedipus legends. His daughter remains unnamed in this drama.

6. Euripides plants here the germ of the possibility that Medea might harm the children, but it is important to stress that the Nurse fears what Medea might do to others, not to the children. She develops this possibility

Her mind is fierce, and she will not endure
ill treatment. I know her. I'm petrified　　　　　　　45
to think what thoughts she might be having now:
a sharpened knife-blade thrust right through the liver—i
she could even strike the royal family, murder
the bridegroom too, make this disaster worse.
She's a terror. There's no way to be　　　　　　　　50
her enemy and come out as the victor.

Here come the children, resting from their games,
with no idea of their mother's troubles.
A child's mind is seldom filled with pain.

*(Enter the Tutor from the house with the two
children of Jason and Medea.)*

TUTOR:
　　Timeworn stalwart of my mistress' household,　　55
　　why do you stand here by the gates, alone,
　　crying out your sorrows to yourself?
　　You've left Medea alone. Doesn't she need you?

NURSE:
　　Senior attendant to the sons of Jason,
　　decent servants feel their masters' griefs　　　　60
　　in their own minds, when things fall out all wrong.
　　As for me, my pain was so intense
　　that a desire crept over me to come out here
　　and tell the earth and sky my mistress' troubles.

TUTOR:
　　Poor thing. Is she not done with weeping yet?　　65

NURSE:
　　What blissful ignorance! She's barely started.

TUTOR:
　　The fool—if one may say such things of masters—
　　she doesn't even know the latest outrage.

---

at 103, but briefly. Medea's later filicidal intentions must come as a relative
surprise.

NURSE:
What is it, old man? Don't begrudge me that.

TUTOR:
70   Nothing. I'm sorry that I spoke at all.

NURSE:
By your beard, don't hide this thing from *me*,
your fellow-servant. I can keep it quiet.

TUTOR:
As I approached the place where the old men
sit and play dice, beside the sacred spring
75   Peirene,[7] I heard someone say—he didn't
notice I was listening—that Creon,
the ruler of this land, intends to drive
these children and their mother out of Corinth.
I don't know if it's true. I hope it isn't.

NURSE:
80   Will Jason let his sons be so abused,
even if he's fighting with their mother?

TUTOR:
He has a new bride; he's forgotten them.
He's no friend to this household anymore.

NURSE:
We are destroyed, then. Before we've bailed our boat
85   from the first wave of sorrow, here's a new one.

TUTOR:
But please, don't tell your mistress. Keep it quiet.
It's not the time for her to know of this.

NURSE:
Children, do you hear the way your father
is treating you? I won't say, *May he die!*

---

7. Peirene, Corinth's sacred spring, ran down from its acropolis.

—he is my master—but it's obvious   90
he's harming those whom he should love. He's guilty.

TUTOR:
Who isn't? Are you just now learning this,
that each man loves himself more than his neighbor?[ii]
If their father doesn't cherish them, because
he's more preoccupied with his own bed—   95

NURSE:
Go inside now, children. Everything
will be all right.

      (The Tutor turns the children toward the house.)

          And you, keep them away—
don't let them near their mother when she's like this.
I've seen her: she looks fiercer than a bull;
she's giving them the eye, as if she means   100
to do something. Her rage will not let up,
I know, until she lashes out at someone.
May it be enemies she strikes, and not her loved ones!

      (In the following passage, Medea sings and the
      Nurse chants.)

MEDEA:

      (From within the house, crying out in rage.)

Aaaah!
Oh, horrible, horrible, all that I suffer,
my unhappy struggles. I wish I could die.   105

NURSE:
You see, this is it. Dear children, your mother
has stirred up her heart, she has stirred up her rage.
Hurry up now and get yourselves inside the house—
but don't get too close to her, don't let her see you:
her ways are too wild, her nature is hateful,   110
her mind is too willful.
          Go in. Hurry up!

(Exit the Tutor and children into the house.)

It's clear now, it's starting: a thunderhead rising,
swollen with groaning, and soon it will flash
as her spirit ignites it—then what will she do?
115   Her heart is so proud, there is no way to stop her;
her soul has been pierced by these sorrows.

MEDEA:
Aaaah!
The pain that I've suffered, I've suffered so much,
worth oceans of weeping. O children, accursed,
may you die—with your father! Your mother is hateful.
120   *Go to hell, the whole household! Every last one.*

NURSE:
Oh, lord. Here we go. What have *they* done—the children?
Their father's done wrong—why should you hate *them?*
Oh, children, my heart is so sore, I'm afraid
you will come to some harm.
                              Rulers are fierce
125   in their temperament; somehow, they will not be governed;
they like to have power, always, over others.
They're harsh, and they're stubborn. It's better to live
as an equal with equals. I never would want
to be grand and majestic—just let me grow old
130   in simple security. Even the *word*
"moderation" sounds good when you say it. For mortals
the middle is safest, in word and in deed.
Too much is too much, and there's always a danger
a god may get angry and ruin your household.

(Enter the Chorus of Corinthian women from the
right, singing.)

CHORUS:
135   *I heard someone's voice, I heard someone shout:*
the woman from Colchis: poor thing, so unhappy.
Is her grief still unsoftened? Old woman, please tell us—
I heard her lament through the gates of my hall.
Believe me, old woman, I take no delight
140   *when this house is in pain. I have pledged it my friendship.*

NURSE:
  This house? It no longer exists. It's all gone.
  He's taken up with his new royal marriage.
  She's in her bedroom, my mistress, she's melting
  her life all away, and her mind can't be eased
  by a single kind word from a single dear friend.   145

MEDEA:
  Aaaah!
  May a fire-bolt from heaven come shoot through my skull!
  What do I gain by being alive?
  Oh, god. How I long for the comfort of death.
  I hate this life. How I wish I could leave it.

                    [Strophe]

CHORUS:
  Do you hear, O Zeus, O sunlight and earth,   150
  this terrible song, the cry
  of this unhappy bride?
  Poor fool, what a dreadful longing,
  this craving for final darkness.
  You'll hasten your death. Why do it?   155
  Don't pray for this ending.
  If your husband reveres a new bed, a new bride,
  don't sharpen your mind against him.
  You'll have Zeus himself supporting
  your case. Don't dissolve in weeping   160
  for the sake of your bedmate.

MEDEA:
  Great goddess Themis and Artemis, holy one:[8]
  do you see what I suffer, although I have bound
  my detestable husband with every great oath?
  May I see him, along with his bride and the palace   165

---

8. The goddess Themis is a Titan (a member of the first generation of gods
born to Gaia and Ouranos, whose names mean "earth" and "sky") and is
closely associated with Zeus' order and hence with justice and law. The
virgin huntress Artemis, daughter of Zeus, presided over important matters such as childbirth and life transitions for women.

scraped down to nothing, crushed into splinters.
He started it. He was the one with the nerve
to commit this injustice. Oh father, oh city,
I left you in horror—I killed my own brother.[9]

NURSE:

170   You hear what she says, and the gods that she prays to:
        Themis, and Zeus, the enforcer of oaths?
        There's no way my mistress's rage will die down
        into anything small.

[Antistrophe]

CHORUS:

        How I wish she'd come outside, let us see
175   her face, let her hear our words
        and the sound of our voice.
        If only she'd drop her anger,
        unburden her burning spirit,
        let go of this weight of madness.
180   I'll stand by our friendship.
        Hurry up, bring her here, get her out, go inside,
        and bring her to us. Go tell her
        that we are her friends. Please hurry!
        She's raging—the ones inside may
185   feel the sting of her sorrow.

NURSE:

        I'll do as you ask, but I fear that my mistress
        won't listen to me.
        I will make the effort—what's one more attempt?
        But her glare is as fierce as a bull's, let me tell you—
190   she's wild like a lion who's just given birth
        whenever a servant tries telling her anything.

        You wouldn't go wrong, you'd be right on the mark,
        if you called them all half-wits, the people of old:

---

9. To slow down the Colchians who were pursuing Medea and Jason after
the theft of the Golden Fleece, Medea killed her younger brother Apsyrtus
and threw his body parts either around the palace at Colchis or at Tomis
on the shore of the Black Sea.

they made lovely songs for banquets and parties,
but no one took time to discover the music   195
that might do some good, the chords or the harmony
people could use to relieve all the hateful
pain and distress that leads to the downfall
of houses, the deaths and the dreadful misfortunes.
Let me tell you, there would be some gain in that—music   200
with the power to heal. When you're having a sumptuous
feast, what's the point of a voice raised in song?
Why bother with singing? The feast is enough
to make people happy. That's all that they need.

(Exit the Nurse into the house.)

CHORUS:
I heard a wail, a clear cry of pain;   205
she rails at the betrayer of her bed,
the bitter bridegroom.
For the injustice she suffers, she calls on the gods:
Themis of Zeus, protectress of oaths,
who brought her to Hellas, over the salt water dark as night,   210
through the waves of Pontus' forbidding gate.[10]

*(Enter Medea from the house, attended by the
Nurse and other female servants. Here spoken
dialogue resumes.)*

MEDEA:
Women of Corinth, I have stepped outside
so you will not condemn me. Many people
act superior—I'm well aware of this.
Some keep it private; some are arrogant   215
in public view. Yet there are other people
who, just because they lead a quiet life,
are thought to be aloof. There is no justice
in human eyesight: people take one look
and hate a man, before they know his heart,   220
though no injustice has been done to them.

---

10. Pontus, literally "The Sea," refers to the Black Sea. As the Chorus sing
of the passage through the Bosporus toward Greece, away from her homeland, Medea passes through the doors of the house.

A foreigner must adapt to a new city,
certainly. Nor can I praise a citizen
who's willful, and who treats his fellow townsmen
225　harshly, out of narrow-mindedness.

My case is different. Unexpected trouble
has crushed my soul. It's over now; I take
no joy in life. My friends, I want to die.
My husband, who was everything to me—
230　how well I know it—is the worst of men.

Of all the living creatures with a soul
and mind, we women are the most pathetic.[11]
First of all, we have to buy a husband:
spend vast amounts of money, just to get
235　a master for our body—to add insult
to injury.[12] And the stakes could not be higher:
will you get a decent husband, or a bad one?
If a woman leaves her husband, then she loses
her virtuous reputation. To refuse him
240　is just not possible. When a girl leaves home
and comes to live with new ways, different rules,
she has to be a prophet—learn somehow
the art of dealing smoothly with her bedmate.
If we do well, and if our husbands bear
245　the yoke without discomfort or complaint,
our lives are admired. If not, it's best to die.
A man, when he gets fed up with the people
at home, can go elsewhere to ease his heart
—he has friends, companions his own age.[iii]

---

11. This presentation of the problems of women in marriage is surprising but not unique in Greek tragedy; a surviving fragment of a lost tragedy by Sophocles, *Tereus,* presents a similar lament by Procne, wife of Tereus. After discovering her husband has raped her sister and cut out her tongue, Procne kills their son and serves his flesh to Tereus as a meal. It is unclear which of these two dramas was produced first.

12. Medea here refers to the dowry that the bride's family had to pay to the groom. Divorce, to which she alludes in the succeeding lines, was a relatively easy procedure for men by filing some papers in court, but almost impossibly complicated for women. On the dowry, see Hippolytus' very different complaint at *Hippolytus* 688–91.

We must rely on just one single soul.   250
They say that we lead safe, untroubled lives
at home while they do battle with the spear.
They're wrong. I'd rather take my stand behind
a shield three times than go through childbirth once.[13]

Still, my account is quite distinct from yours.   255
This is your city. You have your fathers' homes,
your lives bring joy and profit. You have friends.
But I have been deserted and outraged—
left without a city by my husband,
who stole me as his plunder from the land   260
of the barbarians. Here I have no mother,
no brother, no blood relative to help
unmoor me from this terrible disaster.
So, I will need to ask you one small favor.
If I should find some way, some strategy   265
to pay my husband back, bring him to justice,[iv]
keep silent. Most of the time, I know, a woman
is filled with fear. She's worthless in a battle
and flinches at the sight of steel. But when
she's faced with an injustice in the bedroom,   270
there is no other mind more murderous.

CHORUS:
I'll do as you ask.[14] You're justified, Medea,
in paying your husband back. I'm not surprised
you grieve at your misfortunes.
                           Look! I see Creon,
the lord of this land, coming toward us now.   275
He has some new decision to announce.

---

13. The most prominent military tactic in the fifth century BCE was the
hoplite formation whereby heavily armed soldiers would stand closely
together, moving in a tight formation with shields locked together and
spears pointed forward. Athenian adolescents had to swear an oath to the
city in which they promised, among other things, never to leave their position in the line.

14. A promise by the Chorus not to reveal a protagonist's plan was a frequently used device in order to deal with the awkward situation of having
fifteen people present who could divulge to another character what will
happen. Compare *Hippolytus* 786–91.

(Enter Creon from the right, with attendants.)

CREON:
> You with the grim face, fuming at your husband,
> Medea, I hereby announce that you
> must leave this land, an exile, taking with you
280   your two children. You must not delay.
> This is my decision. I won't leave
> until I've thrown you out, across the border.

MEDEA:
> Oh, god. I'm crushed; I'm utterly destroyed.
> My enemies, their sails unfurled, attack me
285   and there's no land in sight, there's no escape
> from ruin. Although I suffer, I must ask:
> Creon, why do you send me from this land?

CREON:
> I'll speak plainly: I'm afraid of you.
> You could hurt my daughter, even kill her.
290   Every indication points that way.
> You're wise[15] by nature, you know evil arts,
> and you're upset because your husband's gone
> away from your bedroom. I have heard reports
> that you've made threats, that you've devised a plan
295   to harm the bride, her father, and the bridegroom.
> I want to guard against that. I would rather
> have you hate me, woman, here and now,
> than treat you gently and regret it later.

MEDEA:
> Oh, god.
> Creon, this is not the first time: often
300   I've been injured by my reputation.
> Any man who's sensible by nature
> will set a limit on his children's schooling

---

15. The Greek adjective *sophê* can mean either "wise" or "clever," and Greek texts, including this one, often play off of this ambiguity. But whether the word's connotation here is closer to wise or clever, Euripides does seem to downplay the traditional representation of Medea as a witch.

to make sure that they never grow too wise.
The wise are seen as lazy, and they're envied
and hated. If you offer some new wisdom   305
to half-wits, they will only think you're useless.
And those who are considered experts hate you
when the city thinks you're cleverer than they are.
I myself have met with this reaction.
Since I am wise, some people envy me,   310
some think I'm idle, some the opposite,ᵛ
and some feel threatened. Yet I'm not all that wise.

And you're afraid of me. What do you fear?
Don't worry, Creon. I don't have it in me
to do wrong to a man with royal power.   315
What injustice have you done to me?
Your spirit moved you, and you gave your daughter
as you saw fit. My husband is the one
I hate. You acted well, with wise restraint.
And now, I don't begrudge your happiness.   320
My best to all of you—celebrate the wedding.
Just let me stay here. I know when I'm beaten.
I'll yield to this injustice. I'll submit
in silence to those greater than myself.

CREON:
Your words are soothing, but I'm terrified   325
of what's in your mind. I trust you less than ever.
It's easier to guard against a woman
(or man, for that matter) with a fiery spirit
than one who's wise and silent. You must leave
at once—don't waste my time with talk. It's settled.   330
Since you are my enemy, and hate me,
no ruse of yours can keep you here among us.

*(Medea kneels before Creon and grasps his hand
and knees in supplication.)*¹⁶

---

16. Supplication was a ritual act through which an individual abased himself
or herself before a more powerful individual by kneeling and grabbing the
latter's knees, often touching his beard as well. Especially in claiming the pro-
tection of the gods, the supplicant's wish should be granted. Medea makes
little headway here until she calls upon Zeus (341), thus raising the stakes.

MEDEA:
>   No, by your knees! By your new-married daughter!

CREON:
>   You're wasting words. There's no way you'll persuade me.

MEDEA:
335 You'll drive me out, with no reverence for my prayers?

CREON:
>   I care more for my family than for you.

MEDEA:
>   How clearly I recall my fatherland.

CREON:
>   Yes, that's what *I* love most—after my children.

MEDEA:
>   Oh, god—the harm Desire does to mortals!

CREON:
340 Depending on one's fortunes, I suppose.

MEDEA:
>   Zeus, do not forget who caused these troubles.

CREON:
>   Just leave, you fool. I'm tired of struggling with you.

MEDEA:
>   Struggles. Yes. I've had enough myself.

CREON:
>   My guards will force you out in just a moment.

MEDEA:
345 Oh please, not that! Creon, I entreat you!

CREON:
>   You intend to make a scene, I gather.

MEDEA:
I'll leave, don't worry. That's not what I'm asking.

CREON:
Why are you forcing me? Let go of my hand!

MEDEA:
Please, let me stay just one more day, that's all.
I need to make arrangements for my exile,   350
find safe asylum for my children, since
their father doesn't give them any thought.
Take pity on them. You yourself have children.
It's only right for you to treat them kindly.
If we go into exile, I'm not worried   355
about myself—I weep for their disaster.

CREON:
I haven't got a ruler's temperament;
reverence has often led me into ruin.
Woman, I realize this is all wrong,
but you shall have your wish. I warn you, though: 360
if the sun god's lamp[17] should find you and your children
still within our borders at first rising,
it means your death. I've spoken; it's decided.
Stay for one day only, if you must.
You won't have time to do the things I fear.   365

(Exit Creon and attendants to the right. Medea
rises to her feet.)

CHORUS:
Oh, god! This is horrible, unhappy woman,
the grief that you suffer. Where will you turn?
Where will you find[vi] shelter? What country, what home
will save you from sorrow? A god has engulfed you,
Medea—this wave is now breaking upon you,   370
there is no way out.

---

17. Creon's threat inadvertently includes Helios, Medea's paternal grandfather, who will help her escape at the end of this drama.

MEDEA:
>Yes, things are all amiss. Who could deny it?
>Believe me, though, that's not how it will end.
>The newlyweds have everything at stake,
375 >and struggles await the one who made this match.
>Do you think I ever could have fawned
>on him like that without some gain in mind,
>some ruse? I never would have spoken to him,
>or touched him with my hands. He's such an idiot.
380 >He could have thrown me out, destroyed my plans;
>instead he's granted me a single day
>to turn three enemies to three dead bodies:
>the father, and the bride, and my own husband.[18]
>I know so many pathways to their deaths,
385 >I don't know which to turn to first, my friends.
>Shall I set the bridal home on fire,[vii]
>creeping silently into their bedroom?
>
>There's just one threat. If I am apprehended
>entering the house, my ruse discovered,
390 >I'll be put to death; my enemies
>will laugh at me.[19] The best way is the most
>direct, to use the skills I have by nature
>and poison them, destroy them with my drugs.
>
>Ah, well.
>
>All right, they die. What city will receive me?
395 >What host will offer me immunity,
>what land will take me in and give me refuge?
>There's no one. I must wait just long enough
>to see if any sheltering tower appears.
>Then I will kill in silence, by deceit.
400 >But if I have no recourse from disaster,
>I'll take the sword and kill them, even if

18. Again, the violence would be directed against Jason, not the children, and the Chorus do not object to actions taken in vengeance against him, Creon, and the bride.

19. Here Medea begins to talk most overtly like a Homeric warrior, obsessed with fame and status, especially in the eyes of "enemies." See Knox, "The *Medea* of Euripides," in Knox (1979), pp. 295–322.

it means my death. I have the utmost nerve.
Now, by the goddess whom I most revere,
Hecate, whom I choose as my accomplice,[20]
who dwells within my inmost hearth, I swear: 405
no one can hurt my heart and then fare well.
I'll turn their marriage bitter, desolate—
they'll regret the match, regret my exile.

And now, spare nothing that is in your knowledge,
Medea: make your plan, prepare your ruse.[21]   410
Do this dreadful thing. There is so much
at stake. Display your courage. Do you see
how you are suffering? Do not allow
these Sisyphean snakes[22] to laugh at you
on Jason's wedding day. Your father is noble;   415
your grandfather is Helios. You have
the knowledge, not to mention woman's nature:
for any kind of noble deed, we're helpless;
for malice, though, our wisdom is unmatched.

CHORUS:

[Strophe 1]

The streams of the holy rivers are flowing backward.   420
Everything runs in reverse—justice is upside down.
Men's minds are deceitful, and nothing is settled,
not even oaths that are sworn by the gods.
The tidings will change, and a virtuous reputation
will grace my name. The race of women will reap   425
honor, no longer the shame of disgraceful rumor.

---

20. The dark goddess Hecate became especially prominent during the fifth
century and was associated with witchcraft and magic.

21. Medea talks to herself, an unprecedented event on the Athenian stage
(at least in the texts that have survived). This device prepares the audience
for her later monologue in which she agonizes over killing her children.
See Foley, "Medea's Divided Self," in Foley (2001), pp. 243–71.

22. Sisyphus of Corinth was notorious for his trickery and deceptiveness,
for which Zeus punished him in Hades by making him push a boulder up
a hill for eternity (*Odyssey* 11.593–600).

[Antistrophe 1]

The songs of the poets of old will no longer linger
on my untrustworthiness. Women were never sent
the gift of divine inspiration by Phoebus
430   Apollo, lord of the elegant lyre,[23]
the master of music—or I could have sung my own song
against the race of men. The fullness of time
holds many tales: it can speak of both men and women.

[Strophe 2]

You sailed away from home and father,
435   driven insane in your heart; you traced a path
between the twin cliffs of Pontus.
The land you live in is foreign.
Your bed is empty, your husband
gone. Poor woman, dishonored,
440   sent into exile.

[Antistrophe 2]

The Grace of oaths is gone, and Reverence
flies away into the sky, abandoning
great Hellas. No father's dwelling
unmoors you now from this heartache.
445   Your bed now yields to another:
now a princess prevails,
greater than you are.

(Enter Jason from the right.)

JASON:
This is not the first time—I have often
observed that a fierce temper is an evil
450   that leaves you no recourse. You could have stayed
here in this land, you could have kept your home

---

23. The epithet *Phoebus* means "shining." Apollo is the leader of the
Muses, the goddesses of music and poetry. The Chorus, of course, ignore
Sappho, a real poetess who would have been unknown to a fictional group
in a story set in the heroic age.

by simply acquiescing in the plans
of those who are greater. You are now an exile
because of your own foolish words. To me
it makes no difference. You can keep on calling   455
Jason the very worst of men.[24] However,
the words you spoke against the royal family—
well, consider it a gain that nothing worse
than exile is your punishment. As for me,
I wanted you to stay. I always tried   460
to calm the king, to soothe his fuming rage.
But you, you idiot, would not let up
your words against the royal family. That's why
you are now an exile. All the same,
I won't let down my loved ones. I have come here   465
looking out for your best interests, woman,
so you won't be without the things you need
when you go into exile with the children.
You'll need money—banishment means hardship.
However much you hate me, I could never   470
wish you any harm.

MEDEA:
                You are the worst!
You're loathsome—that's the worst word I can utter.
You're not a man. You've come here—most detested
by the gods, by me, by all mankind.[viii]
That isn't courage, when you have the nerve   475
to harm your friends, then look them in the face.
No, that's the worst affliction known to man:
shamelessness.
                And yet, I'm glad you've come.
Speaking ill to you will ease my soul,
and listening will cause you pain. I'll start   480
at the beginning. First, I saved your life—
as every single man who sailed from Hellas
aboard the *Argo* knows—when you were sent

---

24. Variations on "worst of men" recur throughout this scene. It inverts
the hero's traditional desire to be called "the best." In the epics of the Trojan War, all heroes vied for this title, often, as in the case of Ajax, at the
cost of their lives.

to yoke the fire-breathing bulls, and sow
485   the deadly crop. I killed the dragon, too:
the sleepless one, who kept the Golden Fleece
enfolded in his convoluted coils;[25]
I was your light, the beacon of your safety.
For my part, I betrayed my home, my father,
490   and went with you to Pelion's slopes, Iolcus—
with more good will than wisdom—and I killed
Pelias, in the cruelest possible way:
at his own children's hands. I ruined their household.

And you—you *are* the very worst of men—
495   betrayed me, after all of that. You wanted
a new bed, even though I'd borne you children.
If you had still been childless, anyone
could understand your lust for this new marriage.

All trust in oaths is gone. What puzzles me
500   is whether you believe those gods (the ones
who heard you swear) no longer are in power,
or that the old commandments have been changed?
You realize full well you broke your oath.

Ah, my right hand, which you took so often,
505   clinging to my knees. What was the point
of touching me?[26] You are despicable.
My hopes have all gone wrong. Well, then! You're here:
I have a question for you, friend to friend.
(What good do I imagine it will do?
510   Still, I'll ask, since it makes you look worse.)
Where do I turn now? To my father's household

25. When Jason asked Medea's father, King Aeëtes, for the fleece, he was
required to yoke these bulls (Medea gave Jason a magic lotion to protect
him from the fire) and sow the ground with the teeth of the serpent Cadmus had killed at the foundation of Thebes. From these teeth sprang
armed men. It is unclear how Medea killed the dragon, and other versions
of the story do not credit her with the actual killing. A vase painting in the
Vatican collection shows Jason half-swallowed by the dragon, with Athena, protector of heroes, standing by watching.

26. In other words, Jason claimed supplication but then ignored his part
of the reciprocal relationship. Oaths were sworn to the gods. To disregard
oaths was thus to commit an offense against the gods.

and fatherland, which I betrayed for you?
Or Pelias' poor daughters? Naturally
they'll welcome me—the one who killed their father!

Here is my situation. I've become   515
an enemy to my own family, those
whom I should love, and I have gone to war
with those whom I had no reason at all
to hurt, and all for your sake. In exchange,
you've made me the happiest girl in all of Hellas.   520
I have you, the perfect spouse, a marvel,
so trustworthy—though I must leave the country
friendless and deserted, taking with me
my friendless children! What a charming scandal
for a newlywed: your children roam   525
as beggars, with the one who saved your life.^ix

Zeus! For brass disguised as gold, you sent us
reliable criteria to judge.
But when a man is base, how can we know?
Why is there no sign stamped upon his body?^27   530

CHORUS:
   This anger is a terror, hard to heal,
   when loved ones clash with loved ones in dispute.

JASON:
   It seems that I must have a way with words
   and, like a skillful captain, reef my sails
   in order to escape this gale that blows   535
   without a break—your endless, tired harangue.
   The way I see it, woman (since you seem
   to feel that I must owe you some huge favor),
   it was Cypris,^28 no other god or mortal,
   who saved me on my voyage. Yes, your mind   540
   is subtle. But I must say—at the risk

---

27. The fifth century BCE saw an increasing concern with the discrepancy between external appearance and internal human nature. See the similar concerns at *Hippolytus* 1028–37.

28. Aphrodite is called Cypris because, after her birth in the sea, she came ashore on the island of Cyprus.

of stirring up your envy and your grudges—
Eros was the one who forced your hand:
his arrows, which are inescapable,
545   compelled you to rescue me. But I won't put
too fine a point on that. You *did* support me.
You saved my life, in fact. However, you
received more than you gave, as I shall prove.[29]
First of all, you live in Hellas now
550   instead of your barbarian land. With us,
you know what justice is, and civil law:[30]
not mere brute force. And every single person
in Hellas knows that you are wise. You're famous.
You'd never have that kind of reputation
555   if you were living at the edge of nowhere.
As for me, I wouldn't wish for gold
or for a sweeter song than Orpheus'[31]
unless I had the fame to match my fortune.

Enough about my struggles—you're the one
560   who started this debate. As for my marriage
to the princess, which you hold against me,
I shall show you how I acted wisely
and with restraint, and with the greatest love
toward you and toward our children—Wait! Just listen![32]
565   When I moved here from Iolcus, bringing with me
disaster in abundance, with no recourse,
what more lucky windfall could I find

---

29. The self-consciously rhetorical style of Jason here would have reminded the audience of the Sophists, the teachers of rhetoric who were prevalent in Athens during these decades. The association would not have been a positive one.

30. Jason ignores that oaths are foundational to a society bound by law. His linkage of lawfulness to Hellenism thus raises the question of who the real "barbarian" is.

31. The son of Apollo and a Muse, Orpheus was a singer with almost miraculous powers. He served as one of Jason's Argonauts. Orpheus was also willing to travel to Hades to save his wife, Eurydice, from death; see the note at *Alcestis* 385.

32. This interjection indicates that Medea must react physically to this outlandish claim.

(exile that I was) than marrying
the king's own child? It's not that I despised
your bed—the thought that irritates you most—   570
nor was I mad with longing for a new bride,
or trying to compete with anyone—
to win the prize for having the most children.
I have enough—no reason to complain.
My motive was the best: so we'd live well   575
and not be poor. I know that everyone
avoids a needy friend. I wanted to raise
sons in a style that fits my family background,
give brothers to the ones I had with you,
and treat them all as equals. This would strengthen   580
the family, and I'd be blessed with fortune.
What do you need children for? For me, though,
it's good if I can use my future children
to benefit my present ones. Is that
bad planning? If you weren't so irritated   585
about your bed, you'd never say it was.
But you're a woman—and you're all the same!
If everything goes well between the sheets
you think you have it all. But let there be
some setback or disaster in the bedroom   590
and suddenly you go to war against
the things that you should value most. I mean it—
men should really have some other method
for getting children. The whole female race
should not exist. It's nothing but a nuisance.[33]   595

CHORUS:
  Jason, you've composed a lovely speech.
  But I must say, though you may disagree:
  you have betrayed your wife. You've been unjust.

---

33. Compare *Hippolytus* 680–87. While the ideology of Greek society
was patriarchal and in many senses misogynistic, it is interesting that, at
least in Athenian tragic drama, men who make such statements wind up
destroyed. On the capacity of the "multivocal" form of Greek tragedy to
overcome the limitations of its society, see Edith Hall, "The Sociology of
Greek Tragedy," in Easterling (1997), pp. 93–126.

MEDEA:

600

605

    Now, this is where I differ from most people.
    In my view, someone who is both unjust
    and has a gift for speaking—such a man
    incurs the greatest penalty. He uses
    his tongue to cover up his unjust actions,
    and this gives him the nerve to stop at nothing
    no matter how outrageous. Yet he's not
    all that wise. Take your case, for example.

610

    Spare me this display of cleverness;
    a single word will pin you to the mat.
    If you weren't in the wrong, you would have told me
    your marriage plans, not kept us in the dark—
    your loved ones, your own family!

JASON:

                         Yes, of course
    you would have been all for it! Even now
    you can't control your rage against the marriage.

MEDEA:

615

    That's not what you were thinking. You imagined
    that for an older man, a barbarian wife
    was lacking in prestige.

JASON:

                    No! Please believe me:
    It wasn't for the woman's sake I married
    into the king's family. As I have said,
    I wanted to save you, and give our children

620

    royal brothers, a safeguard for our household.

MEDEA:

    May I not have a life that's blessed with fortune
    so painful, or prosperity so irritating.

JASON:

    Your prayer could be much wiser: don't consider
    what's useful painful. When you have good fortune,
    don't see it as a hardship.

MEDEA:
                    Go ahead—   625
you have somewhere to turn!—commit this outrage.
I am deserted, exiled from this land.

JASON:
You brought that on yourself. Don't blame another.

MEDEA:
Did I remarry? How did I betray you?

JASON:
You blasphemously cursed the royal family.   630

MEDEA:
And I'm a curse to your family as well.

JASON:
I won't discuss this with you any further.
If you'd like me to help you and the children
with money for your exile, then just say so.
I'm prepared to give with an open hand,   635
and make arrangements with my friends to show you
hospitality. They'll treat you well.
You'd be an idiot to refuse this offer.
You'll gain a lot by giving up your anger.

MEDEA:
I wouldn't stay with your friends, and I would never   640
accept a thing from you. Don't even offer.
There is no profit in a bad man's gift.

JASON:
All the same, I call the gods to witness:
I only want to help you and the children.
But you don't want what's good; you push away   645
your friends; you're willful. And you'll suffer for it.

MEDEA:
Get out of here. A craving for your new bride
has overcome you—you've been away so long.

650   Go, celebrate your wedding. It may be
       (the gods will tell) a marriage you'll regret.

          (Exit Jason to the right.)

CHORUS:

                    [Strophe 1]

       Desire, when it comes on too forcefully, never bestows
       excellence, never makes anyone prestigious.
       When she comes with just the right touch, there's no goddess
              more gracious
       than Cypris.
655   Mistress, never release from your golden bow
       an inescapable arrow, smeared with desire
       and aimed at my heart.

                  [Antistrophe 1]

       Please, let me be cherished by Wisdom, be loved by Restraint,
       loveliest gift of the gods. May dreadful Cypris
660   never stun my spirit with love for the bed of another
       and bring on
       anger, battles of words, endless fighting, strife.
       Let her be shrewd in her judgment; let her revere
       the bedroom at peace.

                    [Strophe 2]

665   O fatherland, O home, never allow
       me to be without a city:
       a grief without recourse, life that's hard to live through,
       most distressing of all fates.
       May I go to my death, my death
670   before I endure that; I'd rather face
       my final day. There's no worse heartache
       than to be cut off from your fatherland.

                  [Antistrophe 2]

       We've seen it for ourselves; nobody else
       gave me this tale to consider.
675   No city, no friend will treat you with compassion

in your dreadful suffering.
May he die, the ungracious man
who won't honor friends, who will not unlock
his mind to clear, calm thoughts of kindness.
I will never call such a man my friend.   680

(Enter Aegeus from the left.) [34]

AEGEUS:
Medea, I wish all the best to you.
There is no finer way to greet a friend.

MEDEA:
All the best to you, Aegeus, son
of wise Pandion. Where are you traveling from?

AEGEUS:
I've come from Phoebus' ancient oracle. [35]   685

MEDEA:
What brought you to the earth's prophetic navel?

AEGEUS:
Seeking how I might beget a child.

MEDEA:
By the gods, are you still childless?

34. Aegeus' is the only entrance from the left in the entire play, which underscores the unexpectedness of his arrival. Aegeus, son of Pandion, is one of the early kings of Athens. He has been visiting the oracle at Delphi in order to learn the cause of his childlessness. A vase painting now in Berlin depicts Aegeus consulting the goddess Themis at Delphi. The son promised at this visit will turn out to be Theseus. In a tragedy that did not survive antiquity, Theseus, Euripides dramatized the story of Theseus' arrival at Athens and the attempt by Medea to kill him because she believed him to be a threat to her position.

35. Apollo's mountainside oracle at Delphi was the most prominent center of prophecy in the Greek world. Sterility was a frequent cause for inquiries by pilgrims there. The "navel" mentioned by Medea is the omphalos, the "navel stone," believed to mark the center of the earth, which was kept on display at Delphi.

AEGEUS:
Still childless. Some god must be to blame.

MEDEA:
690   Do you have a wife, or do you sleep alone?

AEGEUS:
I'm married, and we share a marriage bed.

MEDEA:
Well, what did Phoebus say concerning children?

AEGEUS:
His words were too profound for human wisdom.

MEDEA:
May I hear the oracle? Is it permitted?

AEGEUS:
695   Yes, why not? This calls for a wise mind.

MEDEA:
Then tell me, if indeed it is permitted.

AEGEUS:
He said, "Don't loose the wineskin's hanging foot . . ."[36]

MEDEA:
Before you do what thing? Or reach what place?

AEGEUS:
Before returning to my paternal hearth.

MEDEA:
700   And why have you sailed here? What do you need?

---

36. The leg of the animal-skin wine bag was tied up and then loosened as a spigot for dispensing wine. This phallic image lends itself to a prophecy of the appropriate time for successful intercourse.

AEGEUS:
There is a man named Pittheus, lord of Troezen . . .[37]

MEDEA:
Pelops' son. They say he's very pious.[38]

AEGEUS:
I want to bring this prophecy to him.

MEDEA:
Yes. He's wise, and well-versed in such things.

AEGEUS:
And most beloved of my war companions.　　　　　　705

MEDEA:
Good luck to you. May you get what you desire.

AEGEUS:
But you—your eyes are melting. What's the matter?

MEDEA:
My husband is the very worst of men.

AEGEUS:
What are you saying? Why the low spirits? Tell me.

MEDEA:
Jason treats me unjustly. I've done him no harm.　　　　710

AEGEUS:
What has he done? Explain to me more clearly.

---

37. Pittheus, who understands the prophecy, gives his daughter Aethra to Aegeus after getting him drunk. After Theseus is born at Troezen, he is raised by his mother and Pittheus, who later also raises Hippolytus. See the note at *Hippolytus* 11.

38. Pelops was the son of Tantalus, served by his father as a meal to the gods. After his life was restored, he became the heroic founder of the southern peninsula of Greece, which was then named the Peloponnese, "the island of Pelops," after him.

MEDEA:
He has another wife, who takes my place.

AEGEUS:
No. He wouldn't dare. It's much too shameful.

MEDEA:
It's true. His former loved ones are dishonored.

AEGEUS:
715   Did he desire another? Or tire of you?

MEDEA:
Oh yes, he felt desire. We cannot trust him.

AEGEUS:
Let him go, if he's as bad as you say.

MEDEA:
He desired a royal marriage-bond.

AEGEUS:
Who's giving away the bride? Go on, continue.

MEDEA:
720   Creon, the ruler of this land of Corinth.

AEGEUS:
Woman, your pain is understandable.

MEDEA:
I am destroyed. And that's not all—I'm exiled.

AEGEUS:
By whom? This is new trouble on top of trouble.

MEDEA:
By Creon. He is driving me from Corinth.

AEGEUS:
725   And Jason is allowing it? Shame on him.

MEDEA:
  He claims to be against it, but he'll manage
  to endure it somehow.

  (*Medea again assumes the supplicant position.*)

                    Listen, I entreat you;
  by your beard and by your knees, I beg you:
  Have pity on me; pity my misfortune.
  Don't let me go deserted into exile;   730
  receive me in your home and at your hearth.
  If you do it, may the gods grant your desire
  for children; may you die a prosperous man.
  You don't know what a windfall you have found!
  I'll cure your childlessness, make you a father.   735
  I know the drugs required for such things.

AEGEUS:
  For many reasons, woman, I am eager
  to grant this favor to you: first, the gods;
  and secondly, the children that you promise.
  I'm at a total loss where that's concerned.   740
  But this is how it is. When you arrive,
  I'll treat you justly, try to shelter you.
  However, you must know this in advance:
  I'm not willing to escort you from this land.
  If you can come to my house on your own,   745
  I'll let you stay there—it will be your refuge.
  I will not give you up to anyone.
  But you must leave this land all by yourself.
  My hosts here must have no complaint with me.

MEDEA:
  So be it. But if I had some assurance   750
  that I could trust you, I'd have all I need.

AEGEUS:
  You don't believe me? Tell me, what's the problem?

MEDEA:
  Oh, I believe you. But I have enemies:

Creon, and the house of Pelias.
755 If they come for me, and you're not bound
by any oath, then you might let them take me.
A promise in words only, never sworn
by any gods, might not be strong enough
to keep you from befriending them, from yielding
760 to their delegations. I'm completely helpless;
they have prosperity and royal power.

AEGEUS:
Your words show forethought. If you think it's best,
I'll do it without any hesitation.
In fact, this is the safest course for me:
765 I'll have a good excuse to turn away
your enemies. And things are settled well
for you, of course. I'll swear: just name the gods.

MEDEA:
Swear by the Earth we stand on, and by Helios—
my father's father—and the whole race of gods.

AEGEUS:
770 To do or not do what? Just say the word.

MEDEA:
Never to expel me from your land yourself,
and never, as long as you live, to give me up
willingly to any enemy.

AEGEUS:
I swear by Earth, by Helios' sacred light,
775 by all the gods: I'll do just as you say.

MEDEA:
Fine. And if you don't? What would you suffer?

AEGEUS:
Whatever an unholy man deserves.

(Medea rises.)

MEDEA:
Fare well, then, on your voyage. This is good.
I'll find you in your city very soon,
once I've done my will, and had my way.   780

(Exit Aegeus to the left. The Chorus address him
as he leaves.)

CHORUS:
May lord Hermes, the child of Maia, escort you[39]
and bring you back home. May you do as you please,
and have all you want. In my judgment, Aegeus,
you're a good, noble man.

MEDEA:
O Zeus, and Zeus's Justice, and the light   785
of Helios, I now shall be the victor
over my enemies. My friends, I've set my foot
upon the path. My enemies will pay
what justice demands—I now have hope of this.
This man, when I was at my lowest point,   790
appeared, the perfect harbor for my plans.
When I reach Pallas' city,[40] I shall have
a steady place to tie my ship. And now
I'll tell you what my plans are. Hear my words;
they will not bring you pleasure. I will send   795
a servant to bring Jason here to see me.
When he comes, I'll soothe him with my words:
I'll say that I agree with him, that he
was right to marry into the royal family,
betraying me—well done, and well thought out!   800
"But let my children stay here!" I will plead—
not that I would leave them in this land
for my enemies to outrage—my own children.
No: this is my deceit, to kill the princess.
I'll send them to her, bearing gifts in hand[x]   805
—a delicate robe, and a garland worked in gold.

---

39. Hermes, divine son of Zeus and the nymph Maia, is the protector of
travelers.
40. Medea refers to Athens here. Pallas is one of Athena's epithets.

If she takes these fine things and puts them on,
she, and anyone who touches her,
will die a painful death. Such are the drugs
with which I will smear them.
810   But enough of that.
Once that's done, the next thing I must do
chokes me with sorrow. I will kill the children—
my children. No one on this earth can save them.
I'll ruin Jason's household, then I'll leave
815   this land, I'll flee the slaughter of the children
I love so dearly. I will have the nerve
for this unholy deed. You see, my friends,
I will not let my enemies laugh at me.

Let it go. What do I gain by being alive?
820   I have no fatherland, no home, no place
to turn from troubles. The moment I went wrong
was when I left my father's house, persuaded
by the words of that Greek man. If the gods will help me,
he'll pay what justice demands. He'll never see
825   them alive again, the children that I bore him.
Nor will he ever father another child:
his new bride, evil woman, she must die
an evil death, extinguished by my drugs.
Let no one think that I'm a simpleton,
830   or weak, or idle—I am the opposite.
I treat my friends with kindness, and come down hard
on the heads of my enemies. This is the way to live,
the way to win a glorious reputation.[41]

CHORUS:
Since you have brought this plan to us, and since
835   I want to help you, and since I support
the laws of mankind, I ask you not to do this.

MEDEA:
There is no other way. It's understandable
that you would say this—you're not the one who's suffered.

---

41. Jason has destroyed Medea's identity as a wife. She now in return cancels her maternity, and as part of this process the shift to the language of the male warrior has begun to accelerate over the course of this speech.

CHORUS:
Will you have the nerve to kill your children?

MEDEA:
Yes: to wound my husband the most deeply.   840

CHORUS:
And to make yourself the most miserable of women.

MEDEA:
Let it go. Let there be no more words
until it's done.

(To her attendant.)

You: go now, and bring Jason.
When I need to trust someone, I turn to you.
If you're a woman and mean well to your mistress,   845
do not speak of the things I have resolved.

(Exit the attendant to the right.)

CHORUS:

[Strophe 1]

The children of Erechtheus[42] have always prospered,
descended from blessèd gods.
They graze, in their sacred stronghold, on glorious wisdom,
with a delicate step through the clear and brilliant air.   850
They say that there
the nine Pierian Muses[43] once gave birth
to Harmony with golden hair.

---

42. Athenians. Erechtheus was a legendary early king of Athens. His temple, the Erechtheum, was one of the two most prominent buildings on the Acropolis.
43. The Muses are the children of Zeus and Mnemosynê. Pieria, an important center of worship to the Muses, was often said to be their birthplace.

[Antistrophe 1]

855
They sing that Cypris dipped her pitcher in the waters
of beautiful Cephisus;[44]
she sighed, and her breaths were fragrant and temperate breezes.
With a garland of sweet-smelling roses in her hair
she sends Desires
to take their places alongside Wisdom's throne
860
and nurture excellence with her.

[Strophe 2]

How can this city
of holy rivers,
receiver of friends and loved ones,
receive you—when you've murdered your own children,
865
most unholy woman—among them?
Just think of this deathblow aimed at the helpless,
think of the slaughter you'll have on your hands.
Oh no, by your knees, we beg you,
we beg you, with every plea
870
we can plead: do not kill your children.

[Antistrophe 2]

Where will you find it,
the awful courage?
The terrible nerve—how can you?
How can your hand, your heart, your mind go through with
875
this slaughter? How will you be able
to look at your children, keep your eyes steady,
see them beseech you, and not fall apart?
Your tears will not let you kill them;
your spirit, your nerve will fail:
880
you will not soak your hands in their blood.

(Enter Jason from the right.)

JASON:
I've come because you summoned me. Despite

---

44. Cephisus is one of the two main rivers in Athens.

the hate between us, I will hear you out.
What is it this time, woman? What do you want?

MEDEA:
   Jason, I beg you, please forgive the things
   I said. Your heart should be prepared, receptive   885
   like a seed bed. We used to love each other.
   It's only right for you to excuse my anger.
   I've thought it over, and I blame myself.
   Pathetic! Really, I must have been insane
   to stand opposed to those who plan so well,   890
   to be an enemy to those in power
   and to my husband, who's done so well by me:
   marrying the royal princess, to beget
   brothers for my children. Isn't it time
   to drop my angry spirit, since the gods   895
   have been so bountiful? What's wrong with me?
   Don't I have children? Aren't we exiles? Don't we
   need whatever friendship we can get?
   That's what I said to myself. I realize
   that I've been foolish, that there is no point   900
   to all my fuming rage. I give you credit
   for wise restraint, for making this connection,
   this marriage that's in all our interests. Now
   I understand that you deserve my praise.
   I was such a moron. I should have supported   905
   your plans, I should have made arrangements with you,
   I should have stood beside the bridal bed,
   rejoiced in taking care of your new bride.

   We women—oh, I won't say that we're bad,
   but we are what we are. You shouldn't sink   910
   down to our level, trading childish insults.
   I ask for your indulgence. I admit
   I wasn't thinking straight, but now my plans
   are much improved where these things are concerned.

         (Medea turns toward the house to call the
         children.)

   Oh, children! Come out of the house, come here,   915
   come out and greet your father, speak to him.

Come set aside, together with your mother,
the hatred that we felt toward one we love.

*(The children come out from the house, escorted
by the Tutor and attendants.)*

We've made a treaty. My rage has gone away.
Take his right hand.

920   Oh, god, my mind is filled
with bad things, hidden things. Oh, children, look—
your lovely arms, the way you stretch them out.
Will you look this way your whole long lives?
I think I'm going to cry. I'm filled with fear.
925   After all this time, I'm making up
my quarrel with your father. This tender sight
is washed with tears; my eyes are overflowing.

CHORUS:
In my eyes too fresh tears are welling up.
May this evil not go any further.

JASON:
930   Woman, I approve your new approach—
not that I blame you for the way you felt.
It's only right for a female to get angry
if her husband smuggles in another wife.
But this new change of heart is for the best.
935   After all this time, you've recognized
the winning plan. You're showing wise restraint.
And as for you, my children, you will see
your father is no fool. I have provided
for your security, if the gods will help me.
940   Yes, I believe that you will be the leaders
here in Corinth, with your future brothers.
Grow up strong and healthy. All the rest
your father, with the favor of the gods,
will take care of. I pray that I may see you
945   grown up and thriving, holding sway above
my enemies.

(Jason turns to Medea.)

You! Why have you turned
your face away, so pale? Why are fresh tears
pouring from your eyes? Why aren't you happy
to hear what I have had to say?

MEDEA:

                    It's nothing.
I was only thinking of the children.   950

JASON:
Don't worry now. I'll take good care of them.

MEDEA:
I'll do as you ask. I'll trust in what you say.
I'm female, that's all. Tears are in my nature.

JASON:
So—why go on? Why moan over the children?

MEDEA:
They're mine. And when you prayed that they would live,   955
pity crept over me. I wondered: would they?
As for the things you came here to discuss,
we've covered one. I'll move on to the next.
Since the royal family has seen fit
to exile me (and yes, I realize   960
it's for the best—I wouldn't want to stay
to inconvenience you, or this land's rulers,
who see me as an enemy of the family),
I will leave this land, go into exile,
but you must raise your children with your own hand: 965
ask Creon that they be exempt from exile.

JASON:
Though I may not persuade him, I must try.

MEDEA:
And ask your wife to ask her father: please
let the children be exempt from exile.

JASON:

970   Certainly. I think I will persuade her.

MEDEA:

No doubt, if she's a woman like all others.
And for this work, I'll lend you my support.
I'll send her gifts, much lovelier, I know,
than any living person has laid eyes on:
975   a delicate robe, and a garland worked in gold.[45]
The children will bear them. Now, this very minute,
let one of the servants bring these fine things here.

> (An attendant goes into the house to carry out this request. She, or another servant, returns with the finery.)

She will be blessed a thousandfold with fortune:
with you, an excellent man to share her bed,
980   and these possessions, these fine things that once
my father's father, Helios, passed down
to his descendants. Take these wedding gifts
in your arms, my children; go and give them
to the lucky bride, the royal princess.
985   These are gifts that no one could find fault with.

> (The attendant puts the gifts in the children's arms.)

JASON:

You fool! Why let these things out of your hands?
Do you think the royal household needs more robes,
more gold? Hold onto these. Don't give them up.
If my wife thinks anything of me,
990   I'm sure that I mean more to her than wealth.

---

45. Gold here evokes the Golden Fleece. Medea would destroy her rival
with a token that reminds all of how Jason first won Medea. Spinning and
weaving were, moreover, the activities of the good wife, and Medea here,
like Clytemnestra, uses fabric as the lethal symbol of the dissolution of her
marriage. In Aeschylus' *Oresteia* (*Agamemnon* 905–57), Clytemnestra
spreads out a rich tapestry before Agamemnon and convinces him to walk
on it. She thus proves, among other things, his arrogance.

MEDEA:
  Don't say that. Even the gods can be persuaded
  by gifts. And gold is worth a thousand words.
  She has the magic charm; the gods are helping
  her right now: she's young, and she has power.
  To save my children from exile, I'd give my life,   995
  not merely gold. You, children, when you've entered
  that wealthy house, must supplicate your father's
  young wife, my mistress. You must plead with her
  and ask her that you be exempt from exile.
  Give her these fine things. That is essential: 1000
  she must receive these gifts with her own hands.
  Go quickly now, and bring back to your mother
  the good news she desires—that you've succeeded.

      *(The children, bearing the gifts, leave with the
      Tutor to the right.)*

CHORUS:

                      [Strophe 1]

  Now I no longer have hope that the children will live,
  no longer. They walk to the slaughter already.   1005
  The bride will receive the crown of gold;
  she'll receive her horrible ruin.
  Upon her golden hair, with her very own hands,
  she'll place the fine circlet of Hades.

                    [Antistrophe 1]

  She'll be persuaded; the grace and the heavenly gleam   1010
  will move her to try on the robe and the garland.
  The bride will adorn herself for death,
  for the shades below. She will fall
  into this net; her death will be horrible. Ruin
  will be inescapable, fated.   1015

                      [Strophe 2]

  And you, poor thing, bitter bridegroom, in-law to royalty:
  you don't know you're killing your children,
  bringing hateful death to your bride.
  How horrible: how unaware you are of your fate.

[Antistrophe 2]

1020   I cry for your pain in turn, poor thing; you're a mother, yet
        you will slaughter them, your own children,
        for the sake of your bridal bed,
        the bed that your husband now shares with somebody else.

        *(The Tutor returns, at the right, from the palace
        with the children.)*

TUTOR:
        Mistress, your children are released from exile.
1025   The princess happily received the gifts
        with her own hands. As far as she's concerned,
        the children's case is settled; they're at peace.

        Ah!
        Why are you upset by your good fortune?ˣⁱ

MEDEA:
        Oh, god.

TUTOR:
                    Your cry is out of tune. This is good news!

MEDEA:
        Oh god, oh god.

TUTOR:
1030   Have I made some mistake?
        Is what I've said bad news, and I don't know it?

MEDEA:
        You've said what you have said. I don't blame you.

TUTOR:
        So—why are you crying? Why are your eyes cast down?

MEDEA:
        Old man, I am compelled. The gods and I⁴⁶
1035   devised this strategy. What was I thinking?

---

46. Medea here begins to speak of herself as doing the work of the gods.
The ending of the drama suggests that the gods are in agreement.

TUTOR:
Don't worry now. Your children will bring you home.

MEDEA:
I'll send others home before that day.

TUTOR:
You're not the only woman who's lost her children.
We're mortals. We must bear disasters lightly.

MEDEA:
I'll do as you ask. Now, go inside the house   1040
and see to the children's needs, as usual.

(Exit Tutor into the house.)

Oh, children, children, you two have a city
and home, in which you'll live forever parted
from your mother. You'll leave poor me behind.
I'll travel to another land, an exile,   1045
before I ever have the joy of seeing
you blessed with fortune—before your wedding days,
before I prepare your beds and hold the torches.[47]
My willfulness has cost me all this grief.
I raised you, children, but it was no use;   1050
no use, the way I toiled, how much it hurt,
the pain of childbirth, piercing like a thorn.
And I had so much hope when you were born:
you'd tend to my old age, and when I died,
you'd wrap me in my shroud with your own hands: 1055
an admirable fate for anyone.
That sweet thought has now been crushed. I'll be parted
from both of you, and I will spend my years
in sorrow and in pain. Your eyes no longer
will look upon your mother. You'll move on   1060
to a different life.
                    Oh god, your eyes, the way

---

47. The main event of the Greek wedding ceremony was a nocturnal procession from the house of the bride's family to the groom's. The groom's
mother would greet them bearing a torch.

you look at me. Why do you smile, my children,
your very last smile? Aah, what will I do?
The heart goes out of me, women, when I look
1065   at my children's shining eyes. I couldn't do this.
Farewell to the plans I had before.
I'll take my children with me when I leave.
Why should I, just to cause their father pain,
feel twice the pain myself by harming them?
1070   I will not do it. Farewell to my plans.
But wait—what's wrong with me? What do I want?
To allow my enemies to laugh at me?
To let them go unpunished?
                                             What I need
is the nerve to do it. I was such a weakling,
1075   to let a soothing word enter my mind.
Children, go inside the house.

*(The children start to go toward the house, but, as
Medea continues to speak, they continue to watch
and listen to her, delaying their entry inside.)*

                                             Whoever
is not permitted to attend these rites,
my sacrifice, let that be his concern.
I won't hold back the force that's in my hand.

Aah!
1080   Oh no, my spirit, please, not that! Don't do it.
Spare the children. Leave them alone, poor thing.
They'll live with me there. They will bring you joy.

By the avenging ones[48] who live below
in Hades, no, I will not leave my children[49]
1085   at the mercy of my enemies' outrage.[xii]
Anyway, the thing's already done.
She won't escape. The crown is on her head.

---

48. The Furies, the primordial spirits of vengeance. See the note at line
1289 below.

49. Medea assumes here that Creon's family will kill her children as
would be required by the laws of vengeance. Jason's first words at his final
arrival indicate that she is correct here.

The royal bride's destroyed, wrapped in her robes.
I know it. Now, since I am setting foot
on a path that will break my heart, and sending them   1090
on one more heartbreaking still, I want to speak
to my children.

> (Medea reaches toward her children; they come
> back to her.)

Children, give me your right hands,
give them to your mother, let me kiss them.
Oh, how I love these hands, how I love these mouths,
the way the children stand, their noble faces!   1095
May fortune bless you—in the other place.
Your father's taken all that once was here.
Oh, your sweet embrace, your tender skin,
your lovely breath, oh children.
                              Go now—go.

> (The children go inside.)

I cannot look at them. Grief overwhelms me.   1100
I know that I am working up my nerve[xiii]
for overwhelming evil, yet my spirit
is stronger than my mind's deliberations:
this is the source of mortals' deepest grief.

CHORUS:
Quite often I've found myself venturing deeper   1105
than women do normally into discussions
and subtle distinctions, and I would suggest
that we have our own Muse, who schools us in wisdom—
not every woman, but there are a few,
you'll find one among many, a woman who doesn't   1110
stand entirely apart from the Muses.

Here's my opinion: the childless among us,
the ones who have never experienced parenthood,
have greater good fortune than those who have children.
They don't know—how could they?—if children are pleasant   1115
or hard and distressing. Their lack of experience
saves them from heartache.

But those who have children, a household's sweet offshoot—
I see them consumed their whole lives with concern.
1120 They fret from the start: are they raising them well?
And then: will they manage to leave them enough?
Then finally: all of this toil and heartache,
is it for children who'll turn out to be
worthless or decent? That much is unclear.

1125 There's one final grief that I'll mention. Supposing
your children have grown up with plenty to live on,
they're healthy, they're decent—if fortune decrees it,
Death comes and spirits their bodies away
down to the Underworld. What is the point, then,
1130 if the gods, adding on to the pains that we mortals
endure for the sake of our children, send death,
most distressing of all? Tell me, where does that leave us?

MEDEA:
My friends, I have been waiting for some time,
keeping watch to see where this will lead.
1135 Look now: here comes one of Jason's men
breathing hard—he seems to be about
to tell us of some new and dreadful act.

(Enter the Messenger from the right.)[50]

MESSENGER:
Medea, run away! Take any ship[xiv]
or wagon that will carry you. Leave now!

MEDEA:
1140 Why should I flee? What makes it necessary?

MESSENGER:
The royal princess and her father Creon
have just now died—the victims of your poison.

---

50. The speech by a messenger late in a drama was a convention in Greek tragedy. Such narratives allowed the dramatist to depict spectacular deaths that could not be staged and to include alternative spaces that could not be accommodated within the Greek theater.

MEDEA:
This news is excellent. From this day forth
I'll count you as a friend and benefactor.

MESSENGER:
What are you saying? Are you sane at all,   1145
or raving? You've attacked the royal hearth—
how can you rejoice, and not be frightened?

MEDEA:
I could tell my own side to this story.
But calm down, friend, and please describe to me
how they were destroyed. If you can say   1150
that they died horribly, I'll feel twice the pleasure.

MESSENGER:
When we saw that your two boys had come
together with their father to the bride's house,
all of us—we servants who have felt
the pain of your misfortunes—were delighted;   1155
the talk was that you'd settled your differences,
you and your husband. We embraced the boys,
kissing their hands, their golden hair. And I,
overjoyed as I was, accompanied
the children to the women's quarters. She—   1160
the mistress we now honor in your place—
before she caught sight of your pair of boys
was gazing eagerly at Jason. Then
she saw the children, and she covered up
her eyes, as if the sight disgusted her,[51]   1165
and turned her pale cheek aside. Your husband
tried to cool down the girl's bad temper,
saying, "Don't be hateful toward your loved ones!
Please, calm your spirit, turn your head this way,
and love those whom your husband loves. Receive   1170
these gifts, and ask your father, for my sake,
not to send these children into exile."
Well, when she saw the fine things, she gave in

---

51. Medea's earlier fears about the welfare of her children under a stepmother are confirmed by the new wife's behavior.

1175
to everything the man said. They had barely
set foot outside the door—your children and
their father—when she took the intricate
embroidered robe and wrapped it round her body,
and set the golden crown upon her curls,
and smiled at her bright image—her lifeless double—

1180
in a mirror, as she arranged her hair.
She rose, and with a delicate step her lovely
white feet traversed the quarters. She rejoiced
beyond all measure in the gifts. Quite often
she extended her ankle, admiring the effect.

1185
What happened next was terrible to see.
Her skin changed color, and her legs were shaking;
she reeled sideways, and she would have fallen
straight to the ground if she hadn't collapsed in her chair.
Then one of her servants, an old woman,

1190
thinking that the girl must be possessed
by Pan[52] or by some other god, cried out—
a shriek of awe and reverence—but when
she saw the white foam at her mouth, her eyes
popping out, the blood drained from her face,

1195
she changed her cry to one of bitter mourning.
A maid ran off to get the princess' father;
another went to tell the bride's new husband
of her disaster. Everywhere the sound
of running footsteps echoed through the house.

1200
And then, in less time than it takes a sprinter
to cover one leg of a stadium race,
the girl, whose eyes had been shut tight, awoke,
poor thing, and she let out a terrible groan,
for she was being assaulted on two fronts:

1205
the golden garland resting on her head
sent forth a marvelous stream of all-consuming
fire, and the delicate robe, the gift
your children brought, was starting to corrode

---

52. Pan, half man and half goat, was primarily a pastoral god but also
had associations with violent divine possession and was believed to intervene in battles, causing a terror in enemies that acquired the name
"panic." See also *Hippolytus* 158.

the white flesh of that most unfortunate girl.
She jumped up, with flames all over her,   1210
shaking her hair, tossing her head around,
trying to throw the crown off. But the gold
gripped tight, and every movement of her hair
caused the fire to blaze out twice as much.
Defeated by disaster, she fell down   1215
onto the ground, unrecognizable
to anyone but a father. She had lost
the look her eyes had once had, and her face
had lost its beauty. Blood was dripping down,
mixed with fire, from the top of her head   1220
and from her bones the flesh was peeling back
like resin, shorn by unseen jaws of poison,
terrible to see. We all were frightened
to touch the corpse. We'd seen what had just happened.
But her poor father took us by surprise: 1225
he ran into the room and threw himself—
not knowing any better—on her corpse.
He moaned, and wrapped her in his arms, and kissed her,
crying, "Oh, my poor unhappy child,
what god dishonors you? What god destroys you?   1230
Who has taken you away from me,
an old man who has one foot in the grave?
Let me die with you, child." When he was done
with his lament, he tried to straighten up
his aged body, but the delicate robe   1235
clung to him as ivy clings to laurel,
and then a terrible wrestling match began.
He tried to flex his knee; she pulled him back.
If he used force, he tore the aged flesh
off of his bones. He finally gave up,   1240
unlucky man; his soul slipped away
when he could fight no longer. There they lie,
two corpses, a daughter and her aged father,
side by side, a disaster that longs for tears.

About your situation, I am silent.   1245
You realize what penalty awaits you.
About our mortal lives, I feel the way
I've often felt before: we are mere shadows.

1250   I wouldn't hesitate to say that those
        who seem so wise, who deal in subtleties—
        they earn the prize for being the greatest fools.
        For really, there is no man blessed with fortune.
        One man might be luckier, more prosperous
        than someone else, but no man's ever blessed.

(Exit the Messenger to the right.)

CHORUS:
1255   On this day fortune has bestowed on Jason
        much grief, it seems, as justice has demanded.
        Poor thing, we pity you for this disaster,
        daughter of Creon, you who have descended
        to Hades' halls because of your marriage to Jason.

MEDEA:
1260   My friends, it is decided: as soon as possible
        I must kill my children and leave this land
        before I give my enemies a chance
        to slaughter them with a hand that's moved by hatred.
        They must die anyway, and since they must,
1265   I will kill them. I'm the one who bore them.
        Arm yourself, my heart. Why am I waiting
        to do this terrible, necessary crime?
        Unhappy hand, act now. Take up the sword,
        just take it; approach the starting post of pain
1270   to last a lifetime; do not weaken, don't
        remember that you love your children dearly,
        that you gave them life. For one short day
        forget your children. Afterward, you'll grieve.
        For even if you kill them, they were yours;
1275   you loved them. I'm a woman cursed by fortune.

(Medea enters the house.)[53]

---

53. Medea has been onstage since her first entrance; she has remained through all of the negotiations, meetings, supplications, and choral odes. She finally leaves to commit the horrific murders of her children, and the impact of her departure is intensified by its long delay.

CHORUS:

[Strophe 1]

O Earth, O radiant beam
of Helios, look down and see her—
this woman, destroyer, before she can lay
her hand stained with blood,
her kin-killing hand   1280
upon her own children
descended from you
the gods' golden race;
for such blood to spill
at the hands of a mortal   1285
fills us with fear.
Light born from Zeus,
stop her, remove
this bloodstained Erinys;[54]
take her away   1290
from this house cursed with vengeance.

[Antistrophe 1]

Your toil has all been in vain,
in vain, all the heartache of raising
your children, your dearest, O sorrowful one
who once left behind   1295
the dark Clashing Rocks
most hostile to strangers.
What burden of rage
descended upon
your mind? Why does wild   1300
slaughter follow on slaughter?
Blood-spatter, stain,
slaughter of kin,
murder within
the family brings grief   1305

---

54. Erinys was a Fury, one of the primordial beings born from the castra-
tion of the first king of the gods, Ouranos (sky). The Furies were believed
to punish those who spill kindred blood; hence, in Aeschylus' *Oresteia*,
they pursue Orestes after he kills his mother, Clytemnestra.

tuned to the crime
from the gods to the household.

CHILD:

> *(From within the house.)* [55]

Oh no!

CHORUS:

> [Strophe 2]

Do you hear the shouts, the shouts of her children?
Poor woman: she's cursed, undone by her fortune.

CHILD 1:

1310   Oh, how can I escape my mother's hand?

CHILD 2:

Dear brother, I don't know. We are destroyed.

CHORUS:

Shall I go inside?
I ought to prevent this,
the slaughter of children.

CHILD 1:

1315   Yes, come and stop her! That is what we need.

CHILD 2:

We're trapped; we're caught! The sword is at our throats.

CHORUS:

Poor thing: after all
you were rock, you were iron:
to reap with your own hand
1320   the crop that you bore;
to cut down your kin
with a fate-dealing hand.

---

55. Both of the actors are offstage and thus their voices are available to take the parts of the boys.

[Antistrophe 2]

I've heard of just one, just one other woman
who dared to attack, to hurt her own children:

Ino, whom the gods once drove insane   1325
and Zeus's wife sent wandering from her home.[56]

The poor woman leapt
to sea with her children:
an unholy slaughter.

She stepped down from a steep crag's rocky edge   1330
and died with her two children in the waves.

What terrible deed
could surpass such an outrage?
O bed of their marriage,
O woman's desire: 1335
such harm have you done,
so much pain have you caused.

    (Enter Jason from the right.)

JASON:
    Women, you who stand here near the house—
    is she at home, Medea, the perpetrator
    of all these terrors, or has she gone away?   1340
    Oh yes, she'll have to hide beneath the earth
    or lift her body into the sky with wings
    to escape the royal family's cry for justice.
    Does she think she can murder this land's rulers

---

56. Ino was one of the daughters of Cadmus who participated in the dismemberment of Pentheus while under the spell of Dionysus. She then became the second wife of King Athamas of Iolcus and almost had his sons by his first wife killed (the "evil stepmother" motif again). Hera drove Ino and Athamas mad so that Athamas killed one of the sons Ino had borne to him and Ino leapt into the sea with the other. The Chorus here elide other myths of Greek mothers who kill their children, including Agavê (Ino's sister and Pentheus' mother), Althaea (the mother of the Calydonian hero Meleager), and Procne (see the note at line 232 above). Perhaps this elision is meant to stress the supreme horror of the deed by imagining that only one other could perform it.

1345   then simply flee this house, with no requital?
         I'm worried about the children more than her—
         the ones she's hurt will pay her back in kind.
         I've come to save my children, save their lives.
         The family might retaliate, might strike
1350   the children for their mother's unholy slaughter.

CHORUS:
         Poor man. Jason, if you realized
         how bad it was, you wouldn't have said that.

JASON:
         What is it? Does she want to kill *me* now?

CHORUS:
         Your children are dead, killed by their mother's hand.

JASON:
1355   What are you saying, women? You have destroyed me.

CHORUS:
         Please understand: your children no longer exist.

JASON:
         Where did she kill them? Inside the house, or outside?

CHORUS:
         Open the gates; you'll see your children's slaughter.

JASON:
         Servants, quick, open the door, unbar it;
1360   undo the bolts, and let me see this double
         evil: their dead bodies, and the one
         whom I will bring to justice.

         *(Medea appears above the roof in a flying chariot,
         with the bodies of the children.)* [57]

---

57. As if the scenario were not shocking enough, Medea appears on the
mêchanê, a platform suspended by a crane that was used in the Greek theater typically, if not exclusively, for appearances by gods at a drama's end,

MEDEA:
Why are you trying
to pry those gates? Is it their corpses you seek,
and me, the perpetrator? Stop your struggle.
If you need something, ask me. Speak your mind.   1365
But you will never touch us with your hand.
My father's father, Helios, gives me safety
from hostile hands. This chariot protects me.

JASON:
You hateful thing, O woman most detested
by the gods, by me, by all mankind—   1370
you dared to strike your children with a sword,
children you bore yourself. You have destroyed me,
left me childless. And yet you live, you look
upon the sun and earth, you who had the nerve
to do this most unholy deed. I wish   1375
you would die. I have more sense now than I had
the day I took you from your barbarian land
and brought you to a Greek home—you're a plague,
betrayer of your father and the land
that raised you. But the gods have sent the vengeance   1380
that *you* deserve to crash down on *my* head.
You killed your brother right at home, then climbed
aboard the *Argo* with its lovely prow.
That's how your career began. You married
me, and bore me children. For the sake   1385
of passion, of your bed, you have destroyed them.
No Greek woman[58] would have had the nerve
to do this, but I married you instead:

---

usually to solve crises, tie up loose ends, or denounce humans; hence our use of the Latin translation of this phenomenon, deus ex machina. Euripides was criticized by Aristotle for his reliance on this device, which he also deploys in, among other plays, *Electra, Ion, Iphigenia among the Taurians,* and the *Bacchae.* Medea's violent denunciation of Jason anticipates the similar language of Dionysus toward the Theban royal family at the end of the *Bacchae.*

58. As the Chorus have mentioned (1323–31), there is at least one earlier story of a Greek woman guilty of filicide—and Euripides' audience would have known of others.

1390 a hateful bond. You ruined me. You're not
a woman; you're a lion, with a nature
more wild than Scylla's, the Etruscan freak.⁵⁹
I couldn't wound you with ten thousand insults;
there's nothing you can't take. Get out of here,
you filth, you child-murderer. For me,
1395 all that's left is tears for my misfortune.
I'll never have the joy of my bride's bed,
nor will I ever again speak to my children,
my children, whom I raised. And now I've lost them.ˣᵛ

MEDEA:
I would have made a long speech in reply
1400 to yours, if father Zeus were unaware
of what I've done for you, and how you've acted.
You dishonored my bed. There was no way
you could go on to lead a pleasant life,
to laugh at me—not you, and not the princess;
1405 nor could Creon, who arranged your marriage,
exile me and walk away unpunished.
So go ahead, call me a lion, call me
a Scylla, skulking in her Etruscan cave.
I've done what I had to do. I've jabbed your heart.

JASON:
1410 You feel the pain yourself. This hurts you, too.

MEDEA:
The pain is good, as long as you're not laughing.

JASON:
O children, you were cursed with an evil mother.

---

59. Scylla was a monstrous female giant with twelve feet and six heads, and various canine elements, as described in Books 11 and 12 of Homer's *Odyssey*. She lived opposite the whirlpool Charybdis, and sailors had to choose toward which of the two they would navigate. In the art of the fifth century BCE, Scylla was depicted as an attractive woman above, with a row of dog heads around her waist and a fish tail below. Jason calls her "Etruscan" (in the Greek, "Tyrsenian"), locating her in the Tyrrhenian Sea.

MEDEA:
O sons, you were destroyed by your father's sickness.

JASON:
My right hand is not the one that killed them.

MEDEA:
Your outrage, and your newfound bride, destroyed them.   1415

JASON:
The bedroom was enough to make you kill?

MEDEA:
Does that pain mean so little to a woman?

JASON:
Yes,
to one with wise restraint. To you, it's everything.

MEDEA:
They exist no longer. That will sting you.

JASON:
They exist. They live to avenge your crime.   1420

MEDEA:
The gods know who was first to cause this pain.

JASON:
Oh yes. They know your mind. They spit on it.

MEDEA:
Go on and hate me. I detest your voice.

JASON:
I feel the same. That makes it easy to leave you.

MEDEA:
What shall I do, then? I'd like nothing better.   1425

JASON:
Let me bury their bodies. Let me grieve.

MEDEA:

> Forget it. I will take them away myself
> and bury them with this hand, in the precinct
> sacred to Hera of the rocky heights.
1430
> No enemy will treat their graves with outrage.
> To this land of Sisyphus[60] I bequeath
> a holy festival, a ritual
> to expiate in times to come this most
> unholy slaughter.[61] I myself will go
1435
> to live together with Pandion's son
> Aegeus, in Erechtheus's city.
> And you, an evil man, as you deserve,
> will die an evil death, struck on the head
> by a fragment of the *Argo*.[62] You will see
1440
> how bitter was the outcome of my marriage.

> *(Here the meter changes from spoken dialogue to chanted anapests.)*[63]

JASON:

> May you be destroyed by the children's Erinys
> and bloodthirsty Justice!

MEDEA:

>   What spirit, what god
> listens to you, you liar, you breaker
> of oaths, you deceiver of guests?

---

60. Corinth was the home of Sisyphus, the notorious deceiver; see the note at line 414 above.

61. One of Hera's cult titles in Corinth was *Akraia*, "of the rocky heights," and there was a sanctuary to her by that name there. Pausanias 2.3.6 confirms that there was a sacred festival such as Medea describes here. A number of Euripidean tragedies end with the establishment of a cult; compare *Hippolytus* 1591–1601.

62. Jason will meet an utterly unheroic end, since the hero's goal is a glorious death in battle, not from a rotten piece of a ship.

63. The anapestic meter was often used for exits and thus signals closure. Here the meter also recalls the chanted laments, in anapests, of Medea in the first scene.

JASON:

You are loathsome.
You murdered your children.

MEDEA:

Get out of here, go—
go bury your wife.   1445

JASON:

I'm leaving, bereft
of my sons.

MEDEA:

Do you think that you're mourning them now?
Just wait till you're old.

JASON:
Oh, dearest children.

MEDEA:

To me, not to you.

JASON:
And yet you still did this?

MEDEA:

To make you feel pain.   1450

JASON:
I wish I could hold them and kiss them, my children.

MEDEA:
You long for them now and you want to embrace them,
but you are the one who pushed them away.

JASON:
By the gods, let me touch the soft skin of my children.

MEDEA:
No. What's the point? You are wasting your words.   1455

(The chariot flies away with Medea and the bodies of the children.)

JASON:

Zeus, do you hear how I'm driven away,
do you see what I suffer at her loathsome hands,
this lion, this child-killer!
                                    With all my strength
I mourn for them now and I call on the gods
1460   and spirits to witness that you killed my children
and now won't allow me to touch them or bury them.
I wish now that I'd never fathered them,[xvi] only
to see them extinguished, to see what you've done.

(Exit Jason to the right, accompanied by the Chorus.)

CHORUS:

Zeus on Olympus enforces all things;
1465   the gods can accomplish what no one would hope for.
What we expect may not happen at all,
while the gods find a way, against all expectation,
to do what they want, however surprising.
And that is exactly how this case turned out.[xvii]

Hippolytus

Hippolytus: Cast of Characters

APHRODITE	also called Cypris
HIPPOLYTUS	son of Theseus
CHORUS	of Hippolytus' men
SERVANT	
CHORUS	women of Troezen
NURSE	
PHAEDRA	wife of Theseus and stepmother of Hippolytus
THESEUS	king of Troezen and Athens
MESSENGER	
ARTEMIS	

Hippolytus

SCENE: *Before the palace of Theseus in Troezen, a city*
                across the Saronic Gulf from Athens. A door
                leads into the palace. The stage is flanked by two
                cult statues, one of Aphrodite and one of
                Artemis. Aphrodite appears above the palace.[1]

APHRODITE:
POWERFUL, well-known throughout the earth
and in the heavens, I am the goddess called
Cypris.[2] All who live and see the light
from Pontus to the Pillars of the west[3]
revere my power and receive their due—   5
or, if they scorn me, I can make them pay.
For gods, like men, crave honor and respect;
they revel in the worship they receive.

Soon enough I'll prove that this is true.
Theseus' child, the son of the Amazon,[4]   10

---

1. Aphrodite's appearance above the palace is an informed guess on my part. Most translations have her walk into the acting area through one of the side entrances. But the stress on her power suggests a more vertical orientation that marks the power of the gods. Further, the strong structural symmetries throughout this drama suggest this type of entrance, for Artemis at the end of the play is clearly on the palace roof or on a platform suspended by the crane (see the note at *Medea* 1362, stage direction). Moreover, since Hippolytus' song follows immediately after Aphrodite's last words, a quick withdrawal, which could be accomplished more easily from the roof, seems more plausible than a lengthy departure out of the opposite entrance.

2. Aphrodite. See the note at *Medea* 539.

3. The Black Sea and the Rocks of Gibraltar, also known as the Pillars of Heracles, were the eastern and western boundaries of the known world for the Greeks.

4. After warring against the Amazons, Theseus took one of them as a mate. In mythology she is called either Antiope or Hippolyta, but she is never named in this play. Because of his mother's barbarian status and the nature of her relationship with Theseus, Hippolytus is a bastard.

the protégé of godly Pittheus,[5]
Hippolytus, alone of the citizens
of Troezen, of this land, claims that I am
the very worst of all divinities.

15   He renounces sex, recoils from marriage, honors
only Phoebus' sister, Zeus's daughter
Artemis,[6] whom he believes to be
the very greatest of divinities.
He is with[7] the virgin goddess constantly;

20   racing through the woodlands with his dogs,
he depletes the wild forest of its game
while he enjoys a camaraderie
greater than what mortals might expect.
I don't begrudge the two of them. What for?

25   Where I'm concerned, however, Hippolytus
will find he has miscalculated badly;
and I will make him pay for it, before
this day is out.

          I've cleared the way for what
will happen next; there's little left to do.

30   I set my plan in motion long ago
when Phaedra saw him: once he made a trip
to Athens, from the house of Pittheus,
to see the sacred mysteries and rites;[8]
and she, his father's noble wife, at once

5. Pittheus is the great-grandfather of Hippolytus. His daughter Aethra
gave birth to Theseus after unions with both Aegeus and Poseidon. Theseus, who was raised in Troezen by Aethra and Pittheus before journeying
to Athens to find Aegeus, appears to have sent Hippolytus from Athens to
Troezen to be raised by Pittheus as well. See the note at *Medea* 701.

6. Phoebus is Apollo, the twin brother of Artemis. Aphrodite objects to
Hippolytus' rejection of her in cult worship and his dismissal of the sexual
realm that she rules and represents.

7. "To be with" in Greek, as in English, has sexual overtones. The phrase
marks the incredulity in Aphrodite's attitude toward Hippolytus' relationship with Artemis.

8. The Eleusinian Mysteries were held at Eleusis, very near Athens, in
honor of the goddess Demeter. Initiation into the mysteries was thought to
prepare observers for the afterlife. Note that at the time Hippolytus is ini-
tiated, Phaedra and Theseus are still living in Athens.

felt Desire's dreadful choking grip   35
around her heart, according to my plan.
Before she came to this land, to Troezen,
she founded, right beside Athena's hill,
a shrine to Cypris, overlooking this land,
because of her desire for one who came   40
from far away. Future generations
will say this is the shrine established for
Hippolytus's sake, to Aphrodite. [9]

And now that Theseus has left the land
of Cecrops,[10] and has come here with his wife,   45
in exile for a year, to expiate
his blood-guilt for the sons of Pallas[11]—now
Phaedra suffers badly, feels the lash
of Eros, dread desire; she is destroyed.
She groans, yet will not say the name of her   50
disease. No one in the household knows.

All this will change. It must. I'll make it known
to Theseus—this thing will be revealed.
And this young man, my enemy, will be
killed by his father, who will use the gift,   55
the privilege Poseidon granted: three times
Theseus may call upon the god,
the ocean-lord, who will fulfill his prayers.[12]

---

9. Athena's hill is the Acropolis, which did in fact have such a temple of
Aphrodite, along with a shrine to Hippolytus, both on the south slope
near the Theater of Dionysus. From the south slope one can, on a clear
day, see Troezen across the Saronic Gulf. Athenians fled to Troezen during
the Persian invasion and during the plague.

10. Cecrops was a legendary early king of Athens.

11. Blood-guilt, *miasma*, is incurred for shedding the blood of kin. Pallas,
not to be confused with Athena's epithet, was a half-brother of Aegeus,
and after the death of Aegeus, the sons of Pallas contested Theseus'
assumption of the Athenian throne. He killed them.

12. Like Heracles, Theseus has two fathers, the god Poseidon and the
mortal Aegeus, because his mother, Aethra, had intercourse with both on
the same night. Poseidon had granted his son three *arai*, a word that
means both "prayer" and "curse." The traditional story had Theseus
employing his last, not his first, curse/prayer against Hippolytus; in this

Phaedra may keep her virtuous reputation
60   undiminished; still, she is destroyed.
Her suffering will not deter me from
the vengeance I will take on those I hate.
I'll do what I must do to make it right.

But now I see him: Theseus's son
65   returning from a strenuous morning's hunt—
Hippolytus. And now I must withdraw.
He has a raucous gang of servants with him,
belting out their hymns of adoration
and praise for Artemis.
                                        He doesn't see
70   the gates of Hades gaping wide for him,[13]
or realize this daylight is his last.

*(Exit Aphrodite; enter Hippolytus with Chorus of
Servants from the left.[14] They all sing. A servant
of the goddesses' shrines enters from the palace
and stands near the statues.)*

HIPPOLYTUS:
Follow, follow me, praising
Zeus's heavenly daughter,
Artemis, our protector!

HIPPOLYTUS AND SERVANTS:
75   Mistress on high, Artemis Artemis!
child of Zeus;
hail, beloved

---

play, since he has never tested the *arai,* Theseus is uncertain about his own
paternity.

13. The opening of the gates of Hades and the image that soon follows, of
Hippolytus picking flowers in a meadow (86–97), together suggest the
abduction of Persephone by Hades to be his bride in the *Hymn to Demeter.* The virginity so prized by Hippolytus is not a masculine virtue in
ancient Greece. There is something strangely feminine about Hippolytus;
see the essays on *Hippolytus* in Zeitlin (1996) and Cairns (1997).

14. Unusually, this play has two choruses.

daughter of Leto,
maiden most beautiful!

In the wide sky—Artemis Artemis!—   80
you dwell within
the golden halls
of your father's house,
maiden most lovely
of those on Olympus!   85

HIPPOLYTUS: *(Approaching the statue of Artemis.)*
For you, my Mistress, this elaborate garland
I have woven, from the inviolate meadow
where shepherds do not dare to graze their sheep,
nor has the iron sickle ever cut.
It is inviolate; the honeybee   90
alights there in the spring, and modest Reverence[15]
tends it with the rivulets of dew
for those whose wise restraint is natural
—not studied or instructed, but innate—[16]
who are forever temperate in their souls;   95
such men may pluck the blooms and grasses there,
but those who are impure must stay away.

Receive this braided crown, beloved Mistress
upon your golden hair, from one whose hand
is holy in your service. Only I   100
of all mankind enjoy this privilege:
I may be in your presence, speak and listen;

---

15. Reverence is *aidôs*, an extremely important value that is quite difficult
to translate fully into English. It includes the ideas of reverence, respect,
and shame. The underlying concept is that *aidôs* deters improper behavior. *Aidôs*, reverence, is a key term in this play; see Phaedra's musings at
416–19, for example. For discussions of *aidôs*, see Cairns (1993) and
Woodruff (2001).

16. The debate over the relative roles of nature and nurture was as contested in the fifth century BCE as in our era. Advocates of natural superiority were almost always aristocrats, and antidemocratic. Such language is
likely to have raised some hackles in the mass audience of the Theater of
Dionysus.

I hear your voice, but cannot see your face.
I pray to end my life in just this way.[17]

(The Servant comes forward.)

SERVANT:
105   My lord, since we must call the gods our masters,
would you accept some good advice from me?

HIPPOLYTUS:
Of course. I would not wish to seem unwise.

SERVANT:
Then . . . do you know the rule all mortals follow?

HIPPOLYTUS:
Well—no. What rule is it you have in mind?

SERVANT:
110   That those who act superior are hated.

HIPPOLYTUS:
Yes: arrogance is unendurable.

SERVANT:
And being friendly has a certain charm?

HIPPOLYTUS:
Undoubtedly. And benefit as well.

SERVANT:
Do these same things hold true among the gods?

HIPPOLYTUS:
115   Yes, if our laws mirror the divine.

---

17. The Greek here more literally reads, "May I reach the final turning point of my life just as I began it," which is an allusion to the footraces in the stadion at Olympia. This image was frequently used in the Eleusinian Mysteries.

SERVANT:
Then why do you ignore a holy goddess?

HIPPOLYTUS:
Which one? Be careful, now—watch what you say.

SERVANT:
Cypris! She who stands here by your gate.

HIPPOLYTUS:
I greet her from a distance. I am pure.

SERVANT:
She holds a high position among mortals.   120

HIPPOLYTUS:
"To each his own" holds true for gods *and* men.

SERVANT:
Good luck to you. And may you think again.

HIPPOLYTUS:
I don't like any goddess who's adored at night.

SERVANT:
My child, the gods crave honor. They demand their rights.

HIPPOLYTUS:
Let's go, men.   125
Come inside and see about our meal.
After hunting, nothing can compare
to a full table. And then the horses need
a rubdown, and some good, hard exercise;
I'll yoke them up and take them when I've eaten.   130

(Exiting into the palace with other servants,
acknowledging the statue of Aphrodite.)

As for your Cypris—a fond farewell to her![18]

---

18. "Fond" is sarcastic. Hippolytus' farewell to Aphrodite, even after the
warning from the servant, is remarkably disrespectful.

SERVANT:
     As for me, I know that young men sometimes
     will think that way—they set a bad example.[19]

     (Turning to the statue of Aphrodite.)

135 Mistress, I shall approach you in the manner
     befitting one who is a loyal servant,
     O Cypris. Surely one must be forgiving.
     If someone—some intense, hotheaded youth—
     says something foolish, pretend that you don't hear.
     The gods should be more wise than mortal men.

          *(Exit Servant into the palace. Enter the primary
          Chorus, women of Troezen, from the right.)*

CHORUS:

                    [Strophe 1]

140 There is a place where a stream of Oceanus[20]
     (or so they say) spills out from the rock-face,
     filling the dipping vessels with its water.
     I saw my friend there
     swirling her purple cloths
145 in the gentle rivulets,
     then spreading them out to sun on the stone's flat surface.
     That's where I first heard
     about our mistress

                    [Antistrophe 1]

     wasting away—keeping her body hidden
150 indoors, in sickbed, delicate veils
     shading her chestnut hair. It's been three days now
     she hasn't eaten;

---

19. The servant stresses, as did Aphrodite, the youth of Hippolytus; he is
an ephebe, a young male at the cusp between adolescence and adulthood.
Greek drama is full of such characters, who typically undergo some form
of rite of passage; see Mitchell-Boyask (1999). Note here how the servant
worries about others' copying the risky behavior of Hippolytus.

20. The Greeks believed that the river Oceanus surrounded the world.

she keeps her body pure,
refusing Demeter's gift.[21]
She's suffering from some hidden, tormenting longing   155
to reach her haven,
Death's mournful boundary.

[Strophe 2]

My child, is it Pan
or the sacred Corybantes,
or is it Hecate   160
or the mountain mother[22]
who has cast your mind from its mooring?
Or have you neglected to offer
the ritual cakes
and offended Dictynna, goddess of all wild creatures?[23]   165
She wanders wide
through the salty marsh, and along the bank
that stands amid the swirling ocean waters.

[Antistrophe 2]

Or is it perhaps
the aristocrat, the sovereign   170
of Athens, your husband
is a willing captive
to the secret bed of another?[24]
Or has someone come to the harbor
that welcomes all—   175
someone sailing from Crete,[25] a mariner bringing tidings

21. Food made from grain. Demeter is the goddess of the harvest.

22. Pan is a satyr-like pastoral god; see the note at *Medea* 1191. The Corybantes are the attendants of the mountain mother, the goddess Cybele, whose rites were wild and ecstatic. Hecate is a goddess associated with witchcraft; see also *Medea* 404.

23. Dictynna is a Cretan form of the goddess Artemis.

24. This is the first time the whereabouts of Theseus have been raised. Like his cousin Heracles, Theseus had many adventures during which he had amorous liaisons, so the Chorus raise this possibility not without cause.

25. Phaedra is a Cretan princess, the daughter of King Minos and Queen Pasiphaë.

to make the queen
(in her misery, in her suffering)
a prisoner of grief in her own bedroom?

[Epode]

180   A mournful dissonance
steals into the temperament
of many a helpless woman.
Birthing pangs, delirium—oh child,
that strong wind has darted through my womb.
185   I called on heavenly
Artemis, easer of labor,
mistress of arrows.[26]
Thank the gods, she always comes to me
just when I need her.

(*The Chorus turn toward the palace door, through
which the Nurse and attendants enter, bearing
Phaedra on a couch.*)

190   Look—here comes the old nurse
bringing Phaedra outdoors;
her expression is clouded
with bitter concern.
How my heart is longing
195   to learn what has happened!
What has wrecked the queen's body,
drained her complexion?

NURSE:
Oh, the woes of mankind
and their hateful diseases!
200   What can I do for you? What can I *not* do?
Here's your fresh air, here's your bright sunlight!
Here: we have carried your sickbed outside.
That was all you could talk about—coming out here;
soon enough you'll be wanting to go back inside.

---

26. One of the functions of Artemis was to assist women in childbirth; the death of a woman in childbirth could thus be conceptualized as a fatal attack by the arrows of Artemis.

You keep changing your mind and regretting your choices.   205
You don't want what's in front of you; all that you want
is what you don't have.

It's harder to be a nurse than a patient.
The sick have it easy—they don't have to do much!
But a nurse must endure endless work, endless worry.   210

For the whole human race, life is nonstop disaster,
and there's never a moment of rest from the struggle.
Still, we'd be hard put to say we love anything
more than our lives. If there's anything out there,
it's hidden in darkness, surrounded with clouds.   215
Great fools that we are, we're in love with this flicker—
this unsteady glint of a life—here on earth,
just because we don't know any other existence
or what lies in store for us under the ground.
All we can go by is stories and rumors;   220
it's no use.

PHAEDRA:
              Raise my body up; please, keep my head straight!
My own limbs won't obey me. Servants, come help me:
take my delicate arms, take this veil from my head.
It's too heavy. I want my hair down, on my shoulders.

NURSE:
    Be brave, child, and stop all this wild, restless thrashing!   225
    If you remain calm and remember your breeding,
    you can bear this disease, and not let it oppress you.
    You know that all mortals are burdened with sorrow.

         (The Nurse removes Phaedra's veil.)[27]

PHAEDRA:
    Aah!
    I am longing to draw from the clear streams of dew

---

27. The veil represents the modesty of the married woman. Its removal
here signals the freeing of Phaedra's inhibitions. Herodotus (1.8) preserves
a saying, "A woman takes off her *aidôs* [reverence] with her clothing," a
thought that seems operative here.

230   a pure drink of water, and lay myself down
       in the meadow's deep tresses, beneath the green poplar—

NURSE:
       My child, you are raving! You must stop this public
       careen into madness!

PHAEDRA:
       Let me go to the mountain, ascend to the forest
235   and follow the dogs who are tracking the blood-scent
       of deer through the dapples of light in the pine wood.
       By the gods, let me quench my desire for the cry
       to the pack, for the feel of the hunting-spear flying
       alongside me, grazing my long chestnut hair.[28]

NURSE:
240   My darling, what troubles you? Why this insanity?
       Why should you want to go run with the hounds?
       Your desire for clear water is easily satisfied;
       right by the gate there's a spring, in the hillside.

PHAEDRA:
       Mistress of salt flats, Artemis Artemis!
245   I am longing to ride in your precinct, to master
       the drumbeat of hooves where the horses go running—

NURSE:
       So this is your latest demented pronouncement!
       Just a moment ago you had gone to the mountain
       to indulge in your passion for hunting wild game;
250   now all your desire is to ride on the sandbar,
       skirting along out of reach of the waves.
       What you need is a soothsayer, someone to tell you
       which of the gods has your mind on a tether
       and loves, without warning, to jerk back the chain.

---

28. All of these activities, with their sexualized imagery, are associated
with Hippolytus. Women were expected to remain inside the house at all
times, save for traveling to religious rituals.

PHAEDRA:
Oh no. Oh, how horrible. What have I done.   255
Where on earth did my mind go, in exile from reason?
I was driven insane; I fell into delusion.
Put my veil back in place. Conceal me, please.
I'm ashamed of my words. Please, hide me. My eyes
are choking with tears, distorted with shame.   260
To return to one's wits is unbearable pain.
To be mad is unspeakable. Dying oblivious
is by far the best thing.

NURSE:
I will cover you.

(The Nurse covers Phaedra again with the veil.)

There. But, oh, when will Death
cover *my* body up?   265

I have lived many years, I have learned many things.
When you measure out love, never measure too much;
never let your devotion go deep, to the bone.
We should keep our affection from being too permanent:
if it makes any imprint at all, let it be   270
one that washes right out, so it leaves not a trace.
It's a terrible thing for one soul to endure
someone else's misfortune on top of her own.
And that's what it's been like for me: sick at heart
for her sake.   275

They say that to go through life perfectly steady
and always precise
is a good way to wind up unhealthy, unhappy,
and paying the price.
"Moderation in all things" is what I believe in: 280
"Nothing too much."[29]
Those who have wisdom will vouch for my words.

---

29. These are statements of proverbial wisdom and were found inscribed
on the Temple of Apollo at Delphi. Compare the sentiments of Medea's
nurse at *Medea* 130–34.

CHORUS:
Old woman, trusted servant of the queen,
Phaedra's mournful state is plain to see,
285 but we can't tell from what disease she suffers.
We'd like to learn from you what's wrong with her.

NURSE:
I have no idea. She won't tell.

CHORUS:
Not even how this misery began?

NURSE:
Nothing. She won't breathe a single word.

CHORUS:
290 Her body looks so feeble and exhausted.

NURSE:
No wonder, after three days without food.

CHORUS:
Trying to kill herself? Or is she mad?

NURSE:
If she doesn't eat, her life will end.

CHORUS:
I can't believe her husband lets this happen.

NURSE:
295 She conceals her illness by her silence.

CHORUS:
But can't he tell by looking at her face?

NURSE:
At the moment, he is out of town.

CHORUS:
But—can't you somehow force her to say something?
Can't you try to learn what's made her suffer
and caused her mind to wander helplessly?   300

NURSE:
I've tried everything, and gotten nowhere.
Still, I'm not giving up or losing hope.
You'll see with your own eyes, you'll vouch for me:
I'm steady as a rock when she's in trouble.

(She turns to Phaedra.)

Now, dear child, let's both forget the words   305
we spoke just now. *You* must be more gentle:
let your face relax, let go of that hateful
glare, and change the path that your mind follows.
And I will do my part, and stop pursuing
anything that doesn't seem to help you.   310

If you have some unmentionable illness—
well, these are women. They can help you cure it.
But if it's something you can tell to men,
then speak. You must reveal it to a doctor.

Why are you silent? Silence does no good.   315
My darling, either tell me if I'm wrong
or, if I get it right, agree with me!

Look at me! Say something!
                                It's no use,
my friends; for all the effort that I've made,
we've come no closer—not a single step.   320
She wouldn't listen then, and she still won't:
she can't be soothed, she will not be persuaded.

Just let me say one thing—then go ahead
and be as willful as an ocean wave.
If you die, your children are forsaken.   325
They won't inherit Theseus' estate.
No—I swear by the Amazon, lady of horses,
who bore the one who would be your sons' master,
a bastard who believes himself entitled

330   to legitimate rights—you know the one I mean—
        Hippolytus—[30]

PHAEDRA:

                        Aah, no!

NURSE:

                                His name affects you?[31]

PHAEDRA:
        You've shattered me. I beg you, by the gods,
        never speak of that man ever again!

NURSE:
        You see? You're not delirious, and yet
335   you won't save your own life, or help your children.

PHAEDRA:
        I love my children. Other storms overwhelm me.

NURSE:
        Surely, child, your hands are clear of bloodshed?

PHAEDRA:
        My hands are pure; *miasma* plagues my soul.[32]

---

30. These words say much about the status of Hippolytus: an Amazon's son is almost a paradox in itself because the Amazons generally left their sons for dead. Hippolytus is a bastard but refuses to accept the social limitations this status imposes on him. The question of his "rights" had some contemporary Athenian resonance, since the Periclean citizenship law of 450 restricted the political franchise to legitimate sons. Phaedra's sons are Acamas and Demophon, who later fight in the Trojan War and free their grandmother Aethra from her slavery in Troy.

31. Two changes of speaker in a single line mark this line as highly unusual, and underscore its explosive content.

32. This line echoes Aphrodite's explanation of Theseus' exile (47), but in an extraordinary manner, for *miasma* was purely a matter of external pollution brought about by bloodshed. We see here a growing sense of the complicated depths of human consciousness and the incipient role of intent in determining guilt.

NURSE:
Are you the victim of some hostile magic?

PHAEDRA:
I am destroyed, against my will and his,   340
by a loved one—

NURSE:
Theseus? Has he done you wrong?

PHAEDRA:
I hope that I may never do *him* harm.

NURSE:
Then—tell me! What is driving you to death?

PHAEDRA:
Leave me to go wrong. I'm not wronging you.

NURSE:
Oh no! Not willingly!

(Dropping to her knees and grabbing Phaedra's
hand.)[33]

Don't let me fail!   345

PHAEDRA:
What are you doing? Taking my hand by force?

NURSE:
Your knees as well. And I will not let you go.

PHAEDRA:
This thing is evil. You don't want to learn it.

NURSE:
What could be worse for me than your refusal?

33. The Nurse here resorts to ritual supplication, which requires Phaedra
to consent to her wishes. The continuing contact of the Nurse with Phaedra's body is necessary for the supplication to be effective. Compare
Medea's supplication of Creon, and see the note at *Medea* 332–33.

PHAEDRA:
350   It will kill you—though it brings honor to me.

NURSE:
    Then why on earth conceal it? I'm trying to help you!

PHAEDRA:
    My plans arise from shame, but they are noble.

NURSE:
    Then speaking of them should increase your honor!

PHAEDRA:
    For gods' sake, go away. Release my hand.

NURSE:
355   No. You refuse a gift that you should give.

PHAEDRA:
    I'll give it. I revere your supplication.

NURSE:
    And I shall hold my tongue, and let you speak.

PHAEDRA:
    Poor mother. What a cruel love you desired.

NURSE:
    What do you mean? Her desire for the bull?

PHAEDRA:
360   And you, poor sister, bride of Dionysus.

NURSE:
    Why speak ill of family? What's the matter?

PHAEDRA:
    And I, the third in line. I am destroyed.[34]

---

34. Phaedra chooses a most indirect path for granting the Nurse's request.
She sees herself as the third in a line of Cretan women in love with forbidden

NURSE:
You stun me, child. Where will these words lead?

PHAEDRA:
That's when my agony started, long ago.

NURSE:
I still don't know the answer to my question.   365

PHAEDRA:
If only you could speak the words, not I!

NURSE:
I have no magic power to see what's hidden.

PHAEDRA:
What do people mean when they speak of . . . eros?

NURSE:
The sweetest thing there is—and the most painful.

PHAEDRA:
The latter word would best describe my state.   370

NURSE:
What? My child, are you in love? With whom?

PHAEDRA:
You know—the one you mentioned—the Amazon's . . .

NURSE:
You mean Hippolytus?

PHAEDRA:
                        You spoke his name, not I.

NURSE:
What are you saying, child? You have destroyed me.
Women, this is unbearable, I can't bear   375

---

objects, as her mother Pasiphaë loved the bull and then gave birth to the
Minotaur, and her sister Ariadne the god Dionysus—but only after Theseus,
her first forbidden love, abandoned her on Naxos, which Phaedra omits.

to live. I hate my life, I hate the daylight.
I shall cast down my body, be released
from life. I shall die. Farewell, I exist no longer;
since even those who practice wise restraint
380 desire evil—against their will, no doubt,
but still, they fall in love with what is wrong.
Cypris is no god—I see that now.
She is something greater than a god,
by whose power Phaedra, and myself,
385 and all of us, are one and all destroyed.

(The Nurse exits into the palace.)

CHORUS:
Oh, what was that?
Oh, did you hear
the queen crying out
unspeakable sadness and pain.
390 May I die, my friend, may I die
before I descend
to such a state of mind.
We are under the wing
of hardship, we mortals.
395 You've brought this evil out into the light;
you are doomed; what awaits you this day?
This house will endure
something sudden, unheard of.
We have an inkling now of the unfolding
400 and fading, the outcome
endowered by Cypris.
Poor daughter of Crete.

(Phaedra rises from her couch to address the Chorus.)

PHAEDRA:
Women of Troezen, here on the threshold
of Pelops' land[35]—from time to time I've wondered,
405 thinking far into the night, what is it
that ruins people's lives. When they do wrong,
it seems to me, it isn't through the nature

---

35. Troezen is at the northeastern end of the Peloponnese.

of their minds: most people have good sense.
But you must realize that even though
we know and understand what's right, we fail   410
to act accordingly.[36] Some are just lazy,
and some put other things ahead of goodness—
some other pleasure. Life is filled with pleasures:
endless conversations, the delights
and treacherous indulgences of leisure—   415
and reverence, whose nature is twofold:
one type is good, the other is a burden.
If we could only make a clear distinction,
we wouldn't spell both things with the same letters.[37]

Since I do in fact hold these opinions,   420
no drug or magic spell could make me change
my way of thinking. Let me now describe
the path that my mind followed to arrive here.

When love first wounded me, I tried to think
of how to bear this thing with dignity.   425
My first idea, therefore, was to hide
my state in silence—conceal my disease.
(The tongue cannot be trusted: it knows how
to give advice to other people's minds,
but on its own it brings you only trouble.)   430

I then took care to bear this madness well:
to overcome it, using wise restraint.

But after that, when these approaches failed
to break the hold that Cypris had on me,
then, it seemed, the most effective plan—   435
my only recourse, really—was to die.

36. This thought seems to respond to the Socratic argument that people
never do wrong willingly, that knowledge of the truth will always lead to
the correct action. Socrates was a contemporary of Euripides. Phaedra's
words are not a direct challenge to the philosopher but feed off of arguments that would have been circulating in the world of the theater audience.
37. The ambiguity of this passage has caused much scholarly ink to be
spilled. How reverence, *aidôs*, is a pleasure is very unclear, unless it is such
to one for whom it is an overriding concern; Artemis, for example, calls
virginity a pleasure (1455).

For just as I would want the world to know
if I did something good, I couldn't bear
the public eye if I did something shameful.
440 I knew that this disease was a disgrace,
no less than the act, and I knew well
that I was a woman—an object of contempt
to all.

I wish an evil fate on her—
that woman who was first to bring disgrace
445 to her own bed, with other men! This spread
from the nobility, and now infects
all females. When good families begin
to practice what is shameful, certainly
the base will think there's dignity in evil.

450 And I detest those women who pretend
to practice wise restraint: their words are pure;
their hearts are filled with secret insolence.
How can they—Cypris, mistress of the ocean!—
how can they look their husband in the eye
455 untrembling, unafraid that their accomplice
the darkness, or the house's very timbers,
will suddenly speak out?

—This, my friends,
is why I must die; so that I may never
be found to bring disgrace upon my husband
460 or upon the children that I bore.
Let them live and thrive in Athens, honored
in that glorious city, unencumbered
by shame on my account. Let them be free
and speak out openly, as free men do.
465 Even a tough-minded man becomes
slavish when he knows some evil thing
about his mother or father. The only way
to win in life, they say, is to be honest
and have good judgment. Time betrays the base;
470 it holds the mirror up to them, as if
to a young girl. May I never be seen
casting such an image of myself.

CHORUS:
Ah, wise restraint is always dignified;
the fruit it bears is glorious renown.

(The Nurse enters again from the palace.)

NURSE:
Mistress, the troubles you were speaking of   475
just now had me terribly upset and frightened.
But now I'm thinking: what a simpleton
I was! Second thoughts, you know, sometimes
show the wiser way; we're only human.
This thing you're suffering from can be explained,   480
it's not all that unusual. The goddess
has sent her anger crashing down on you.
You are in love—what's so strange about that?
So are many others. Why on earth
should you die because of desire? If everyone   485
who ever desired someone had to die—
well, what would be the point of that?

                              The goddess
Cypris has the power of a flood tide;
she's overwhelming. Those who yield to her
she will pursue more calmly; those who scorn her   490
or those who are unusually proud—
you can't imagine how she crushes them.

Cypris wanders through the upper air;
she is in the ocean wave. All things on earth
come from her, the sower of desire,   495
whose children we all are. And anyone
who has the writings of the ancient poets
and takes a special interest in the Muses
knows how Zeus desired Semele
once upon a time,[38] and lovely Eos   500

---

38. This mythological paradigm does not bear scrutiny. Zeus' desire
for Semele led to her death when she asked him to appear to her in his
real form, lightning, which incinerated her, and Zeus pulled the fetus
of Dionysus from her body. The Chorus provide this information at
618–27.

took Cephalus to live among the gods
because of her desire.[39] Still, the gods
go on living in the sky; they don't
go into exile; no, they make their peace
505   with their erotic troubles and defeats.

And you cannot hold up? Well, then, your father,
when he begot you, should have made some special
arrangement for you, so that you could live
on different terms, with different gods as masters,
510   if you can't make your peace with these conditions.

Do you have any idea how many men
with excellent good sense, whose marriages
are ailing, still pretend that they don't see?
How many fathers help their sons go wrong,
515   connive with Cypris? Here's a piece of wisdom:
if something isn't good, the world's eyes
must turn away from it. Don't waste your time
working for perfection in your life:
You wouldn't labor over every detail
of the roof above your head.

520   You've fallen in
to such bad luck—do you have any idea
how to swim back out? You're only human,
so if the good you have outweighs the bad,
you're doing pretty well.

                     But, oh, my child,
525   stop this evil thinking, and give up
this arrogance—yes, that's what it is,
arrogance, to want to overcome
what is divine. Now, as for your desire:
be brave. A god has engineered these things.
530   If you are ailing, there must be some way
to get the best of this, and make it well.
There are spells, and magic incantations;
we will find some drug for this disease.

---

39. Eos is the goddess of the dawn and Cephalus is an Athenian. Eos is
also said to have taken the Trojan Tithonus as a lover, but she forgot to
ask for his eternal youth when Zeus granted him immortality.

We women are the quickest to discover
the ways that men find slowly, if at all.   535

CHORUS:
Phaedra, her advice is certainly
more practical, considering your troubles.
But you're the one I praise—although I know
these words may be more painful to your ears.

PHAEDRA:
This is what destroys whole populations—   540
good cities and good homes—attractive words!
The point of speech should not be mere delight,
but how to earn a virtuous reputation.

NURSE:
Well, aren't you superior! But, Phaedra,
what you need is not high-sounding talk: 545
you need that man. The undiluted truth
must be known and spoken right away.
If you were not in so much trouble, if
you were managing your life with wise restraint,
then I would never push you to this point   550
just to bring some pleasure to your bedroom.
But, child, the thing at stake here is your *life*.
I'm trying to save it. Don't begrudge me that!

PHAEDRA:
Just close your mouth. Don't say another word.
Please, no more of this dreadful, shameful talk!   555

NURSE:
Shameful, maybe, but you're better off
listening to me if it will save you.
Where your survival is concerned, the act
is worth more than your precious reputation.

PHAEDRA:
Don't go any further, please, for gods' sake!   560
Your words are so persuasive and so shameful,
and my soul is so receptive—Desire has

prepared it like a seedbed—if you keep on,
I'll succumb to what I'm trying to escape.

NURSE:
565   All right. If that seems best to you . . . Of course,
you shouldn't be going wrong like this at all,
but as things are, the second-best resort
is for you to trust me. I just now remembered
that I have certain charms at home, to soothe
570   desire, to put an end to this disease
without danger to your senses, or anything
to be ashamed of—if you have the courage.

We need something from him—the one you love—
a strand of hair, or something that he wears,
575   some token to commingle with the charm
to bring about a favorable result.

PHAEDRA:
Will this drug be an ointment or a drink?

NURSE:
Oh, I don't know, my child. Just let me help you.

PHAEDRA:
I am afraid that you are much too clever.

NURSE:
580   Then you are much too nervous. What's your fear?

PHAEDRA:
That you will mention this to Theseus' son.

NURSE:
Don't worry, darling. I will make things right.

And you, O Cypris, mistress of the ocean,
be my ally and accomplice now.
585   The rest of what I have in mind, I'll tell
to friends within the house. That will suffice.

(Exit Nurse into the palace. Phaedra remains.)

CHORUS:

[Strophe 1]

Eros, Eros, melting desire in the eyes,
sweet delight in the souls
of all your victims,
come to me never, never if not in peace;   590
never upset my mind,
dance with me out of time.
Shafts of fire, piercing light of the stars
cannot compare with the bolt
of Aphrodite;   595
the bolt you fling from your hands,
Eros, child of Zeus.

[Antistrophe 1]

No use, no use, the heaps of slaughtered cattle
that Greece in her abundance
brings to Delphi,   600
brings to Olympia[40]—yet we forget
to placate Eros, the tyrant,
Eros, who holds the keys
to Aphrodite's most intimate chamber: Love
the destroyer, whenever he comes   605
to visit mortals;
he flings his victims down
through every type of ruin.

[Strophe 2]

The filly of Oechalia, unbroken,
who never had known marriage bed, or man,   610
was taken from her father's home
under the yoke—
a runaway nymph, a bacchante;
in blood and smoke,
a marriage of carnage,   615

---

40. Delphi, sacred to Apollo, and Olympia, sacred to Zeus, were the two
most important centers of worship in the Greek world.

Cypris gave her to Alcmene's child.
O heartbreaking wedding.[41]

[Antistrophe 2]

O sacred walls of Thebes, O mouth of Dirce,
you could tell of Cypris' sly approach:
620   she wraps the bride in the bloodstained arms
of her fate.
The mother of twice-born Bacchus
she made the mate
of fire-flanked thunder.[42]
625   She rages like a gale, and then, like a bee
she flies away lightly.

PHAEDRA: *(Listening at the palace door.)*
Be quiet, women. We are done for now.

CHORUS:
What dreadful thing have you just heard inside?

PHAEDRA:
Wait—let me listen—let me hear that voice.

CHORUS:
630   I will be quiet. But, oh, this is a prelude
to something terrible, I can tell.

PHAEDRA:
                                        Aah, no!
I am defeated. Oh, what misery!

---

41. Heracles became so besotted with Iole's beauty that he destroyed
Oechalia when her father refused to give her to him. Heracles sent her to
his home as a slave, not telling his wife, Deianira, his real purpose for her,
a deception that brought about his death. This myth is the subject of
Sophocles' *The Women of Trachis* and is hinted at in Bacchylides 5.

42. Thebes was the home of Semele, and Dirce was its main river. Bacchus
(Dionysus) was twice-born because he was taken from the burning body
of his mother, Semele, sewn into Zeus' thigh, and then born later from the
body of his father.

*(In the following passage, the Chorus sing in
dochmiacs and Phaedra speaks.)*

CHORUS:
What are you saying, Phaedra?
What is this cry of grief?
Tell me, what words, what words   635
have shaken your senses so?

PHAEDRA:
We are destroyed. Come hear this cataclysm
for yourself. Come listen at the door.

CHORUS:
You are already there.
You are the one to tell   640
what has been said within.
Tell me now, tell me, what
terrible thing has occurred?

PHAEDRA:
It is the son of the equestrienne,
the Amazon—Hippolytus. He's shouting   645
at my servant, flaying her with words.

CHORUS:
I can hear him shouting, but what's it about?
Speak to me: what kind of cry
comes to you through the gates?

PHAEDRA:
His words are very clear. He's calling her   650
whoremonger, traitor to her master's bed.

CHORUS:
Oh, this is bad for us.
You are betrayed, my friend.
What can I do that will help you?
What was hidden is revealed, and you are ruined,   655
betrayed by those closest to you!

PHAEDRA:
She has destroyed me by naming my disaster.
A well-meaning, evil-doing, would-be healer.

CHORUS:
What will you do, since there is no way out?

PHAEDRA:
660   There's only one way. I must die as soon
as possible; that is the only cure.

(Enter Hippolytus and Nurse through the palace
door. Phaedra withdraws to the rear of the acting
area and listens.)

HIPPOLYTUS:
O mother Earth, and open, sunlit sky!
Unspeakable—the things that I have heard!

NURSE:
Be quiet, child! What if someone hears you?

HIPPOLYTUS:
665   I can't be silent in the face of this.

NURSE:
I beg you, by your beautiful right arm—[43]

HIPPOLYTUS:
Let go of my hand! Don't touch my clothes!

NURSE:
I beg you, by your knees! Oh, I am done for!

HIPPOLYTUS:
How's that? I thought you said that this was nothing
to be ashamed of—

---

43. The Nurse attempts to repeat her supplication of Phaedra, which
Hippolytus will not allow. Nevertheless, she has already secured an oath
from him.

NURSE:

It's a private matter!   670

HIPPOLYTUS:
If it's decent, you should want the world to know.

NURSE:
My darling, do not violate your oath.

HIPPOLYTUS:
My tongue is bound by oath, but not my mind.

NURSE:
Oh, child, do not destroy those closest to you!

HIPPOLYTUS:
No one so depraved is close to me!   675

NURSE:
Please be forgiving.
It's only human to go wrong, my child.

HIPPOLYTUS:
Zeus! What made you plague all men on earth
with this affliction, brass disguised as gold—
women! If it was to propagate   680
the species, couldn't you have found a way
for this to be accomplished without wives?[44]
Men could go and place within your temples
a quantity of bronze, or iron, or gold
to pay for children—every man assessed   685
according to his means—then we'd be free
to live in peace, without the female sex![i]

I can prove that woman is an evil.
The father who engendered her and raised her

---

44. The breathtaking misogyny of this speech typifies attitudes in fifth-
century BCE Athens and, indeed, has deep roots in Greek culture, as seen
in Hesiod's myth of Pandora (*Theogony* 570–613, *Works and Days* 57–
105).

690   pays off a bribe when he gets rid of her:
the dowry, as a consolation prize!
The man who takes this evil piece of work
into his house delights in decking out
his idol in the finest robes and jewels—
695   the poor fool, wasting all the wealth he has.[ii]
If the object of his worship is some brainless
nobody—well, that's bad enough:
she's good for nothing, but he has it easy.
A clever woman, on the other hand,
700   is something I detest. May that type never
set foot inside my house: a female thinker.
For Cypris has bestowed on clever women
more than their share of criminality.
An imbecilic woman is at least
705   saved from folly by her helplessness.

A woman should be kept away from servants
and spend her time with inarticulate
wild beasts, so she can neither speak
nor hear the sound of any other voice.
710   But as it is, they sit inside and plot
their evil schemes, which servants carry out—
the way you are right now! How dare you come
to me, suggesting that I violate
the sanctity of my own father's bed?
715   You abomination! I must go
to purify my ears with flowing water.
How could you think that I could be so base?
To me, the words alone are a pollution!

My piety is all that's saving you.
720   If you had not entrapped me with an oath,
I would have told my father every word.
Now, as it is, I'll stay away as long
as Theseus is absent from this land,
and I will hold my tongue. But just as soon
725   as he returns, I'll come back to observe
how you can bear to look him in the eye,
you and your mistress.[iii] To hell with both of you!
My loathing for you is insatiable—
women! I don't care if I'm accused

of repeating myself endlessly, since they   730
are capable of endless wickedness.
If they can't learn to practice wise restraint,
then I can't stop excoriating them.[45]

(Exit Hippolytus to the right.)

NURSE:[iv]
Oh, what a bleak
unhappy fate   735
we women are born to.
What word now, what ruse will undo
what our words have knotted us into?
O sunlight and Earth,
our sentence is passed down.   740
How can I get away?
How can I hide this pain?
What god will help me now? What mortal would
ever want to appear to be my
accomplice in these   745
depraved deeds? I am done for.
My misery will spill above the rim,
outlive its container;
my life here is over.
Poor woman, poor me.   750

CHORUS:

(Turning to Phaedra.)

Ah, mistress, it is finished now. Your servant's
ruses have gone wrong. All is in ruins.

PHAEDRA:

(She now steps forward and speaks to the Nurse.)

How utterly and absolutely you
have done me in, you loathsome woman, how

---

45. There is considerable irony in this violent denunciation of women for
lacking restraint. Compare Phaedra's last words (810–11).

755   unlike a friend, to destroy me! May the bolt
           of Zeus, my ancestor,[46] scorch you to dust!
           Did I not say, did I not make it clear
           (knowing *you*) that you were to say nothing?
           But that was too much for you. Now I've lost
760   the virtuous name that I was meant to die with.

           I need a new plan. Knowing him, the way
           his mind is sharpened now with rage, he'll tell
           his father *your* misdeeds—at my expense.
           He'll tell old Pittheus of my disaster.
765   He'll fill this land with lacerating words.
           To hell with you, and every would-be friend
           who drives the knife in, thinking it will help!

NURSE:
           Mistress, you have every right to blame
           me for these troubles—the injury you feel
770   has overcome your judgment. If I may,
           however, I would like to tell my side.
           I raised you, and I care for you. I tried
           to cure your illness, but the drug I found
           did not work out the way it was supposed to.
775   If it had worked, you'd say I was a genius.
           When everything goes well, we call it wisdom.

PHAEDRA:
           Surely you don't imagine that these words
           could possibly suffice for what you've done.

NURSE:
           Well, we've gone on too long. It's true that I
780   lacked wisdom, and restraint. But there's still hope,
           my darling—

PHAEDRA:
                        Quiet! Just stop talking! You've
           done harm enough already with your bad
           advice and all the evil you've attempted.

---

46. Zeus was the father of Phaedra's father, Minos.

Just go and mind your own affairs, and I
will see to mine; yes, I will make things right.   785

(Exit Nurse into the palace; Phaedra turns to the
Chorus.)

Children of Troezen's most noble families,
my friends, I ask one favor only: please
keep all that you have heard wrapped up in silence.[47]

CHORUS:
By Artemis on high, the child of Zeus,
I swear that I will keep your troubles hidden   790
and never bring them out into the light.

PHAEDRA:
Well-spoken. I have one more thing to add.
I've found a way, in spite of this disaster,
to benefit myself and help my children
preserve their honor and their reputation.   795
I never will disgrace the land of Crete,
nor will I ever look into the eyes
of Theseus with scandal on my name.
I will not be deterred by one small life.

CHORUS:
What evil and incurable recourse   800
do you intend to take?

PHAEDRA:
                  I'm going to die.
But I must plan exactly how.

CHORUS:
                       Don't say that!

PHAEDRA:
Don't try to dissuade me. I shall be

---

47. There are now two oaths of silence. After Phaedra's suicide, Hippolytus cannot defend himself to his father, nor can the Chorus explain to Theseus what has happened.

805   a source of great delight and satisfaction
        to Cypris, my destroyer, by my death
        before this day is out. The bitterness
        of Love prevails, and I shall be defeated.
        But I shall do great evil to that man
        by dying—he will share in my disease,
810   not place himself above me; he will learn
        to practice wise restraint, when all is done.[48]

        (Exit Phaedra into the palace.)

CHORUS:

[Strophe 1]

        Let me hide beneath[49]
        the smooth recesses of the looming cliffs;
        I would become
815   a bird, if only a god would give me wings,
        and soar beyond
        the Adriatic waves, to reach the place
        where tears of pity, gleaming amber drops
        spill from the brimming eyes of Phaethon's
820   poor, heartbroken sisters
        into the violet stream.[50]

[Antistrophe 1]

        The Hesperides,
        enchanting singers, tend their apple trees
        far to the West;
825   let me arrive at the limit of the sky,

---

48. Phaedra echoes the final denunciation from Hippolytus (732–33).

49. Euripides was fond of such "escape odes," in which a chorus expresses its desire to flee from the coming disaster by evoking a series of mythological paradigms.

50. Phaethon, like Hippolytus an ephebic charioteer, is the son of Helios who asks his father for proof of his paternity in the form of permission to drive the sun god's chariot. The ride proves fatal to Phaethon. His sisters, in the extremity of their grief for him, are changed into poplar trees by the gods, weeping amber.

which Atlas holds,
where sailors reach the final boundary
the sea-lord keeps, upon the violet wave,
and streams forever flow, where Zeus once lay,
where Earth pours her treasure   830
out for the blessed gods.[51]

[Strophe 2]

Ship with white wings
sailing from Crete,
salt-battered hull
bringing her here   835
from a good home—
unlucky bride!
It was to be a disastrous marriage.
Terrible portents
coming and going: 840
leaving her homeland,
reaching the mainland;
stepping ashore at
glorious Athens,
knotting the hawsers—   845
birds of ill omen
greeted the sailors.

[Antistrophe 2]

Then she was trapped;
sent by the dread
goddess of love   850
like a disease,
impure desire
shattered her mind.
Battered by grief, from her bridal chamber's

---

51. The Hesperides are nymphs who guarded the golden apples given to
Zeus and Hera at their wedding by Gaia (Earth). Atlas, the Titan punished
by Zeus with eternally holding up the sky, tells Heracles where to find the
Hesperides in one of Heracles' final labors. The reference to Earth, after
the Hesperides, suggests that "where Zeus once lay" indicates the love-
making of Zeus and Hera after their wedding.

855   sheltering roof-beam,
        Phaedra will fasten
        onto her white neck
        her final mooring—
        feeling the shame of
860   hateful misfortune,
        saving her good name,
        cleansing her mind of
        painful desire.

NURSE:

(From within.)

        Help, help!
        Everyone around the house—come quickly!
865   She's hanging by a rope—our mistress—Theseus' wife!

CHORUS:
        Ah, it is finished now. The queen is dead:
        a woman dangling by a knotted noose.

NURSE:
        Won't you please hurry? Someone bring a sharp
        iron blade, to cut this knot around her neck.

CHORUS MEMBER:
870   What should we do, friends? Should we rush inside
        to free our mistress from that stranglehold?

CHORUS MEMBER:
        But aren't there servants—aren't there men nearby?
        It's never wise to be too meddlesome.

NURSE:
        Lay straight her broken body. How I grieve.
875   This is a task that fills my heart with pain.

CHORUS:
        She's dead, unhappy woman; that is clear.
        They're speaking now of laying out her corpse.

*(Enter Theseus from the left; he is wearing a
garland, since he is returning from the shrine of
an oracle.)* [52]

THESEUS:
　Women, what was that? I heard a shout
　of servants from inside. It sounded grim;
　and no one's here to give me the reception   880
　that I expected: open doors, and smiles
　to welcome the returning pilgrim home.
　I hope old Pittheus is safe from harm—
　not done in by some freshly sprung disaster.
　He's gotten on in years, I know, but still   885
　his passing from this house would bring me grief.

CHORUS:
　This stroke of fortune does not touch the old,
　poor Theseus. It is the young who are cut down.

THESEUS:
　Not one of my children. Oh, my god.

CHORUS:
　They live; their mother's death is bitter pain.   890

THESEUS:
　What are you saying? My wife? How did she die?

CHORUS:
　She slipped a knotted noose around her neck.

THESEUS:
　What happened? Did some sorrow chill her heart?

CHORUS:
　That's all we know. I've just arrived myself,
　to find that I am now your fellow-mourner.   895

---

52. The garland recalls the wreath Hippolytus brought onstage and gave
to Artemis.

THESEUS:
A pilgrim's homecoming!

> *(He tears the garland from his head and throws it to the ground.)*

What good is this?
Why bind my accursèd head with woven stems?
Servants, let the doors be opened wide;
undo the bolts, and let me see this terror:
900   my wife, who has destroyed me with her death.

> *(The doors are opened and Phaedra's body is revealed. A wooden tablet is attached to her wrist. Theseus and the Chorus sing in lyric meters.)*[53]

CHORUS:
Oh, my poor Phaedra, no!
How you have suffered, how
completely you've undone your household—
how could you be so rash?
905   What has happened? Why this violent fall,
this grapple with yourself, which you have lost,
this unholy deed?
Who doused your life in darkness?

THESEUS:

[Strophe]

Oh, this is agony.
910   How I have suffered, how
intensely this surpasses all the pain
I've ever felt before.

---

53. The body of Phaedra would have been made visible through the use of the *ekkyklêma*, a cart designed to display bodies quickly from inside the house. The tablet would have been a hinged piece of wood with a coating of wax on its inner panels. Messages were written on the wax, which could be rubbed to erase the letters when no longer needed.

Some evil fortune infiltrates my house,
infects me like an ancient, blood-borne curse![54]

This is the end for me.   915
I have no life; instead,
I see an ocean, endless waves of pain
through which I cannot swim, nor reach the shore.

What are the words for this?
How can I name your fate?   920
You vanished like a bird out of my hands,
hurtling down to Hades, out of sight.

Agony, agony.
Some primal sin, some long-ago offense
has come at last to settle in my arms: 925
the gods' penalty.

CHORUS:
My lord, this pain is not unique to you.
Many men have lost beloved wives.

THESEUS:
                    [Antistrophe]

Darkness beneath the earth
let me descend, and dwell   930
deep in the shadows, in the land of death,
now that I've lost your love,
Phaedra, my companion, my destroyer;
yours is not the only life you've shattered.

What brought about your fate?   935
What did your heart sustain?
Will someone tell me, or are all of you
a useless mob beneath your master's roof?

Oh, how I grieve your loss.
Misery for this house   940

---

54. It is unclear what curse might be involved here, and this reference
might be simply commonplace. Theseus might be thinking of his *miasma*
for the blood of the sons of Pallas, or perhaps his role in the death of his
father, Aegeus.

unspeakable, unbearable; I am
destroyed, our home is empty, motherless.

You've left us; you're gone,
dear friend, most precious woman here beneath
945   the sun's bright eye, the nighttime's steady gaze
flashing with stars.

CHORUS:
Poor Theseus. This poor house
bears such a weight of pain.
Tears are flooding my eyes.
950   I shudder, I tremble to think
what misery follows on this.

THESEUS:[55]
Ah! What's this?
Here is a tablet dangling from the wrist
of my dear wife. What news does it contain?
Poor woman, it may be that she's concerned
955   about our children and our marriage bed.
Poor Phaedra. Please don't worry: Theseus
will never bring another woman home.

(He examines the tablet.)

Here's the impression of her golden ring,
the seal of one who now exists no longer.
960   It clutches at my heart. Let me unwrap
these laces, break the seal—I must know
what this tablet has to say to me.

CHORUS:
Oh no, no. The gods
send fresh evil now
965   hard on the heels of her death.[v]
This house no longer exists:
it is destroyed, destroyed.[vi]

_____

55. Theseus now stops singing and returns to the meters of speech.

THESEUS:
    Oh, agony. Oh, pain on top of pain,
    unbearable, unspeakable. Oh, agony.

CHORUS:
    Tell me—what? If I may know this thing.   970

THESEUS:
    This tablet shouts aloud
    terrible, dreadful words.
    Where can I run to, where
    can I escape this crushing weight, this pain?
    I'm dead. I am destroyed.   975
    This song, the writing's voice
    is venom to my eyes.

CHORUS:
    Your words blaze out an open swath of pain.

THESEUS:
    I can no longer hold in
    these words that I bite back.   980
    They lacerate me as I speak.
                        O citizens!
    Hippolytus has laid his hand by force
    upon my marriage bed, a violation,
    an outrage to the sacred eye of Zeus!

    Poseidon, O my father, once you promised   985
    that I would have the power of three curses.
    I want to use one now: annihilate
    my son, and let him die before this day
    is out. Show me that you have promised truly.

CHORUS:
    My lord, by all the gods, take back that prayer.   990
    Believe me, soon enough you'll realize
    that you've done wrong—

THESEUS:
                        No, absolutely not.
    And what is more, I hereby exile him

from this land. One cruel fate will strike him down
995   or else the other: Poseidon will respect
my curse, and hurl him to the land of death,
or else he'll live a broken wanderer
far from here, and end his days alone.[56]

(Enter Hippolytus from the right, attended by
companions and servants.)

CHORUS:
Look, here's your child now—Hippolytus
1000   in person, just in time. Please, Theseus,
my lord, give up your cruel anger—think
of what will do your household the most good.[57]

HIPPOLYTUS:
Father, I heard your shout and came at once.
What's going on? I'd like to hear from you
1005   what's wrong, the reason for your cries of grief.
Ah, what's this?
                Father, it's your wife—
dead! This thing astounds me. I am stunned.
Just now I left her, in this very daylight,
just recently! Tell me—what is going on?
1010   What destroyed this woman? Father, please:
I'd like to learn from you what happened to her.

No answer? Please, this is no time for silence.
Not when you're in trouble. The heart desires
knowledge, craves each detail, even in
1015   the worst misfortune. Father, it's not right
to hide your sorrows from the ones you love.

---

56. Theseus, unsure whether Poseidon really is his father, here covers himself in case there are in fact no curses. He now seems to forget about the curses until the arrival of the messenger.

57. What follows here is essentially a trial scene, with Theseus as the prosecutor and Hippolytus the defendant. This kind of stylized debate was called an *agon* and bore the marks of the growing influence of formal rhetoric on the courts of Athens.

THESEUS:
  Oh, the human race! How stupidly
  and blindly we go wrong, time and again!
  For all our boundless ingenuity,
  our great inventions and discoveries,   1020
  there's still one prize we can't hunt down and trap:
  the gift of thought for empty-headed dolts!

HIPPOLYTUS:
  Yes, that would be a brilliant tour de force,
  to teach the empty-headed how to think.
  But, Father, this is inappropriate,   1025
  beside the point—this finely polished speech.
  Are your misfortunes causing you to rave?

THESEUS:
  If only there were some reliable
  criterion, some foolproof way to judge
  the inner thoughts of people close to us,   1030
  to tell who is your friend and who is not!
  And everyone should have two separate voices:
  the natural one, whatever it may be,
  and then another, always honest one.[58]
  That way, the voice with secret thoughts of harm   1035
  could be exposed by one that says what's right,
  and we would never be deceived.

HIPPOLYTUS:
                              Wait—
  Has someone close to you contaminated
  my name with accusations? I've done nothing!
  Father, I'm astounded—it's as if   1040
  your words have lost all contact with your sense—

THESEUS:
  Sense!? I'll tell you what the human mind
  will stop at—nothing! There's no limit, no
  depravity mankind will not attempt!

---

58. Compare Phaedra's remarks about two kinds of reverence (416–19).

1045   If man's audacity intensifies
        as time goes on, if each new generation
        is more outrageous than the one before,
        the gods will have to add more land to earth
        to make more room for all these misbegotten
1050   criminals! Just look at him—my own
        son! He has disgraced my marriage bed,
        and this poor woman's body proves his utter
        perversity.

                    (Hippolytus covers his face.)

                            Come here, and show your face
        to your own father.[59] Go ahead and do it!
1055   Your presence has infected me already.

        So, you're the paragon of wise restraint,
        the man so holy, so inviolate
        that gods are his companions? So you boast—
        as if the gods had no more sense than that!

1060   You think that you're so pure. Well, go ahead
        and tout the marvels of a meatless diet!
        Go worship Orpheus and Dionysus![60]
        Revel like a madman! Go ahead,
        bring out those worthless, gaseous, sacred texts!
        I have you now.
1065   The rest of you, take note:
        watch out for men like this. They're arrogant,

---

59. In his first version of this story, Euripides appears to have had Hippolytus veil his head in horror when Phaedra tried to seduce him. It is unclear exactly how Hippolytus hides his face here, whether simply by turning away or by using some article of clothing. I suggest in my 1999 essay, "Euripides' *Hippolytus* and the Trials of Manhood (The *Ephebia*?)," that Hippolytus covers himself with a cloak that was typically worn by ephebes in Athens. The veiling here also recalls Phaedra's earlier in the drama.

60. It is clear here how little Theseus understands his son, save that he is different from him. Hippolytus' first appearance in the play had him arranging a feast with his men after a hunt. Orpheus and Dionysus were worshiped in mystery cults and thus could be names hurled gratuitously against someone claiming to have a special connection to a god.

they try to sound superior and holy,
but they will hunt you down and do you harm.

She's dead. Do you think that will save you? No:
that proves your guilt the most of all, you monster.   1070
What words, what oath could possibly compare
with her? How can you possibly escape
this accusation?
                    No doubt you will say
she hated you: a bastard child is always
at odds with those who are legitimate.   1075
Oh yes, that was good thinking on her part,
to give her life up for some petty grudge!

Or, you will claim, *men* don't lose their heads;
only women are susceptible.
Well, I've seen young men fall apart like girls   1080
when Cypris stirs their minds with thoughts of sex.
At that point, they're just lucky that they're male.[61]

And therefore—wait: why should I waste my time
debating with you? Here's the evidence:
her body! There can be no testimony   1085
more foolproof.
                    Leave this land right now, at once.
Your exile has begun. Stay out of Athens,
the city built by gods; stay far away
from any land protected by my spear!
If you think you can get away with this,   1090
then Sinis of the Isthmus will deny
that I'm the man who killed him, and the rocks
of Sciron, by the sea, will say that I'm
no threat to criminals, an empty boaster.[62]

CHORUS:
    I would not say that human happiness   1095
    exists. The greatest can be overturned.

---

61. Theseus himself, one of the more notorious philanderers in Greek myth, knows this subject all too well.

62. Sinis and Sciron were bandits killed by Theseus during his heroic first journey from Troezen to Athens when he was the same age as Hippolytus is now.

HIPPOLYTUS:
Father, the sheer force of your attack,
your mind's intensity, is staggering.
As for the case itself, you're well supplied
1100 with pretty words, but when you look inside
it's not so pretty.

I'm no orator:
I have no gift for speaking to a crowd;
I'm much more clever in small groups, with friends
my age, who share my interests. Naturally:
1105 people who speak poorly to a clever,
well-educated audience are often
quite eloquent in front of a huge throng.[63]

At any rate, I am compelled to speak
in view of this disaster. I shall start
1110 with your first accusation, which you thought
would take me by surprise and bring me down
with no defense.
                    Well—if your eyes can see
the daylight, and the world around you—know
that in this world there is no man alive
1115 whose wisdom and restraint surpass my own,
even if you say it isn't true.[64]

For I know, first of all, that one must honor
the gods; and secondly, I choose my friends
with care, avoiding those who might attempt
1120 an unjust act: an innate sense of reverence
prevents a decent man from doing wrong,
or getting someone else to do wrong *for* him,
or dealing shamefully with those around him.

I'm faithful to those close to me: I'd never

---

63. Such denials of skill at speaking were common in ancient oratory; see, for example, the opening of Socrates' first speech in Plato's *Apology*. However, Hippolytus' denial has a special edge as it continues to assert his elitist outlook.

64. Bound by his oath, Hippolytus can only argue from probability (i.e., why he is unlikely to have attempted to rape his stepmother), another commonplace of rhetoric.

act one way when they're with me, and then sneer   1125
and mock them when they're not around.

                                And, Father,
there's one thing I have never done, the very
thing you think you've caught me in: my body
is pure and untouched; I have never known
erotic love, up to this very moment,   1130
except to hear descriptions and to look
at pictures—even that I'd really rather
avoid, because my mind and soul are chaste.

All right. I see that you are not persuaded
by my capacity for wise restraint.   1135
Never mind. But you must then explain
what could have made me stoop to such an act.
Was it because her body and her looks
were so much lovelier than other women's?
Or maybe I was hoping to usurp   1140
your place by taking possession of your wife.
In that case, I had truly lost my mind.
Is power sweet to men of wise restraint?
No, not at all, unless these power-lovers
have taken leave of all their common sense.^{vii}   1145
As for me, I'd like to take first place
competing in the Panhellenic games,⁶⁵
but in the city I prefer to have
a secondary role, surrounded by
people of good quality; for me,   1150
that's happiness enough to last forever:
the opportunity without the danger
of royal power.⁶⁶

                There's just one more thing

---

65. The great cycle of athletic festivals at Olympia (Olympic Games), Corinth (Isthmian Games), Delphi (Pythian Games) and Argos (Nemean Games).

66. In other words, Hippolytus has no desire for participation in the affairs of the city. It is unlikely that such values would have been approved by the audience in Athens, which prized devotion to the common good through service to the city.

I have to say, and then I'll rest my case.
1155   If I had any witness here to tell
what sort of person I am, and if *she*
were still alive and saw the light of day,
then you would know for certain who is wrong.
As things are, I can only swear to you
1160   by Zeus the god of oaths, and by the earth
beneath our feet: I never touched your wife;
I never wanted to; it never crossed
my mind. May I die utterly unknown
and unremembered,[viii] may the earth and sea
1165   refuse to shelter so much as my corpse,
if I'm a criminal by disposition.

What she was afraid of, why she took
her own life, I don't know. It is not right
for me to say more. She showed wise restraint
1170   when she could not restrain herself. And I
was able to—though I have paid the price.

CHORUS:
Your oaths should be sufficient to deflect
this accusation: the gods stand by your words.

THESEUS:
I ask you: have you seen a smoother charlatan—
1175   a sideshow conjurer by disposition!
He's outraged his own father, and he thinks
he'll get the best of me by keeping calm!

HIPPOLYTUS:
Father, I am equally amazed
at you. If you were the child, and I the father,
1180   I would have killed you, not just sent you off,
if you had laid a hand upon my wife.

THESEUS:
Oh, that's just *like* you! Don't think you'll die
like that, so easily, on your own terms.
A man in trouble wants a rapid death.
1185   But you will live a broken, wandering exile
far from here, and end your days alone.[ix]

HIPPOLYTUS:
What are you doing? Won't you even wait
for time to bring in evidence against me
before you drive me out?

THESEUS:
                    I'd send you farther
than Pontus or the Pillars of the west[67]   1190
if I could. That's how much I hate you.

HIPPOLYTUS:
You won't consider oaths, or solemn pledges,
or prophecies, before you throw me out
without a trial?

THESEUS:
                    This tablet here is solemn
pledge and evidence enough against you.   1195
As for prophecy, and little birds
above our heads—a fond farewell to them![68]

HIPPOLYTUS:
Oh, gods, why don't I speak right here and now,
since you destroy me in my piety?
But no—he wouldn't believe me anyway;   1200
I'd only break in vain the oath I swore.

THESEUS:
This arrogant superiority
is killing me! Why don't you leave right now:
leave your fatherland!

HIPPOLYTUS:
                    Where will I turn
in exile, poisoned by this accusation?   1205
What host will ever take me in? I'm ruined.

---

67. Theseus' words here echo Aphrodite's at the play's opening (4).
68. Theseus echoes Hippolytus' impious insult to Aphrodite (131).

THESEUS:
>Try finding someone who appreciates
>a guest who comes in and corrupts his wife!

HIPPOLYTUS:
>That hurts me. I feel close to tears. Do you
1210
>honestly believe that I'm so bad?

THESEUS:
>The time to think this through was *then*, before
>you did this outrage to your father's wife.
>Now it's too late to cry.

HIPPOLYTUS:
>   I wish this house,
>these walls, could speak for me, could truly say
1215
>if I'm a criminal by disposition.

THESEUS:
>A witness who can't speak—oh, very clever!
>But you're convicted by the concrete facts.

HIPPOLYTUS:

>*(Groans.)*

>If only I could stand outside myself
>and shed free-flowing tears at what I see,
>at this injustice—

THESEUS:
1220
>   As it is, you spend
>far too much time in rapt self-adoration
>and not enough in honoring your parents!

HIPPOLYTUS:
>My poor mother. Oh, my birth was bitter.
>I hope those close to me will all be spared
>the pain of being a bastard—

THESEUS:
1225
>   Servants! Now!

Are you listening? Take this man away.
You heard me. He's no longer a citizen.

HIPPOLYTUS:
Anyone who touches me will be sorry.
Throw me out yourself, if that's what you want.

THESEUS:
I will, if you won't listen. I don't feel   1230
even the slightest pity for your exile.

HIPPOLYTUS:
Well, then. It's decided. And yet I know,
sadly, all I know, but cannot say.

(He turns to the statue of Artemis.)

Most beloved goddess, child of Leto,
companion, fellow-hunter: we shall leave   1235
glorious Athens. Farewell to that city,
dominion of Erechtheus.[69] Farewell
to you, Troezen, a joyful place to live
when one is young. This is the last time
I'll ever see you.
          Young men, come with me,   1240
come say good-bye, and lead me from this land.
For you will never see another man
whose wisdom and restraint surpass my own,
although my father doesn't seem to think so.

*(Exit Hippolytus with companions to the left.
Exit Theseus into the palace.)*

HIPPOLYTUS' SERVANTS:

[Strophe 1]

The thought that the gods care at all about us   1245
brings me tremendous relief from affliction.
Still, when I hold out hope

69. A legendary early king of Athens. See the note at *Medea* 847.

that I ever will understand human life, or a mortal's
chances for happiness, I'm left with nothing.
1250   Everything changes from day to day; it's impossible
to stand on a patch of ground that will not shift.

CHORUS:

[Antistrophe 1]

If only the gods would respond to my prayers,
here's what I'd ask for: first, to be happy;
then for a spirit unscathed,
1255   inviolate, free from pain; and a mind that is not too
overprecise, but not misguided either.
Let me be easy and changeable, and from day to day
attempt in my way to grasp at happiness.

HIPPOLYTUS' SERVANTS:

[Strophe 2]

Things that I never had hoped for have happened; my thoughts
are no longer
1260   clear, no longer calm, for we have seen him,
the brightest star of Hellas, leave this land
in hurt and in haste, all because of his father's anger.
White sand of the shore, deserted strand of our city,
Deep tangle of forest, woodlands where once he went hunting,
1265   his dogs outracing him, and by his side
holy Dictynna.[70]

CHORUS:

[Antistrophe 2]

Never again will you ride with your team on the salt flats, no
longer
hold the twining reins, and hear the drumbeat
of horses' hooves. The music that once poured
1270   all night in the halls of your father will now be silent.

---

70. A Cretan goddess closely associated with, if not identical to, Artemis.
See line 165 and note.

The places where Artemis rests in the cool green forest
will no longer be draped with garlands; no longer will young girls
compete so tenderly to be your bride,
now that you've left us.

[Epode]

As for me, I'll flood the world with tears   1275
lamenting your unhappy fate.
You were born for nothing, nothing;
ah, your poor mother.
I am enraged at the gods.
Sweet Graces, twining arms in your lovely dance,   1280
how can you send this poor man away
from his home, his fatherland?
He has done nothing, nothing.
His mind is innocent of all this ruin.

(Enter a messenger from the left.)

CHORUS:
    Look: one of Hippolytus's men   1285
    is hurrying this way. His face looks grim.

MESSENGER:
    Women, can you tell me where to look for
    Theseus, the ruler of this land?
    Is he inside the palace? If you know
    please tell me.

CHORUS:

(Gesturing to the palace door.)

                There. He's coming outside now.   1290

MESSENGER:
    Theseus, the news I bring is bad
    for you and for the citizens of Athens,
    as well as those who live here in Troezen.

THESEUS:

    What is it? Has there been some fresh disaster
1295   that touches both of my close-allied cities?

MESSENGER:

    I'll put it simply: Hippolytus no longer
    exists. That is, he's hanging by a thread.

THESEUS:

    Who killed him? Did he rape somebody's wife,
    the way he did his father's, and incur
    somebody's violent hatred?

MESSENGER:

1300   His own chariot
    destroyed him, and the prayers that you yourself
    pronounced against your son, when you called down
    the curses of the ocean-lord, your father.

THESEUS:

    O gods!
           And O Poseidon! After all,
1305   you truly are my father, since you heeded
    my prayers.
           How did it happen? How did Justice
    bring her deadfall down to crush his head
    for what he did to me?

MESSENGER:

    We were by the shore, where ocean waves
1310   come rolling in to shelter on the sand.
    And as we groomed the horses, we were weeping.
    For we had been informed that by your order
    Hippolytus was exiled from this land,
    poor man. Then he himself came down to meet us
1315   there at the shore, with all his followers,
    friends his own age, an enormous crowd.
    He confirmed the words to this lament,
    this song awash in tears.
                After a while
    he'd had enough of crying, and he spoke:

1320   "Why should I be distressed? My father's words

must be obeyed. Servants, yoke the fillies[71]
to the chariot. I can no longer
call this city my own."

           Then every man,
faster than you could say the words, performed
his task; the team was harnessed, ready,   1325
presented to our master. He took up
the twining reins and set his feet in place.
He raised his hands in prayer, and spoke these words:

"O Zeus, may I no longer see the daylight
if I'm a criminal by disposition.   1330
But whether I die or live, I pray my father
may come to know how he dishonors me."

With that, he took the whip and struck the fillies
expertly. And we servants kept our pace
beside the chariot which held our master   1335
standing tall, and we attended him
along the road which leads to Epidaurus
and Argos.[72] When we reached the empty stretch
beyond the borders of this land, we saw
the promontory there that stretches out   1340
into the Saronic Gulf. And then
the earth began to growl, like Zeus's thunder,
rising to a roar that set our hair on end.
Each horse's ears shot straight up in the air,
each neck stretched taut. We were beside ourselves: 1345
what was that sound?
           We looked up toward the cape,
and from the pounding surf we saw emerge
a wave, unearthly, swallowing the sky:
I couldn't see the coast of Sciron, or
the Isthmus, or Asclepius's rock.[73]   1350

---

71. It is perhaps significant that the horses of Hippolytus, which will soon
destroy him in their panic, are female.

72. Argos is to the west, and Epidaurus to the northwest, of Troezen. The
Saronic Gulf is the body of water between Athens and Troezen.

73. Sciron, one of the bandits Theseus killed, lived along the coast. The Isthmus is the stretch of land connecting the Peloponnese to northern mainland

Spurting foam, the breaker arched and swelled
as it approached the chariot on shore,
and from its liquid sinews it expelled
a bull, a wild portent.[74] All the earth
1355   was saturated with its monstrous voice.
The echoes were enough to freeze our nerves;
the sight of it was more than we could bear.

Stark terror struck his mares that very instant.
Our master, who for many years has known
1360   the ways of horses, pulled back on the reins
with all his weight, the way a sailor throws
his body backward pulling on an oar.
But they just took the fire-hardened bit
between their teeth, and pulled him on by force,
1365   unmindful of the chariot, the reins,
or of their steersman. When he turned the helm,
directing them to where the ground was softer,
the bull appeared in front of them, and drove
the fillies mad with fear, and made them run
1370   the other way. But when they dashed insanely
toward the rocks, the bull stole silently
alongside them, close by the twining reins
until he finally smashed the chariot
against the crag, its outer wheels splintered,
1375   a shattered heap. The axles and the pins
went flying; meanwhile, tangled in the reins,

Greece. The rock of Asclepius is obscure, but perhaps meaningful. Hippolytus is headed toward Epidaurus, the traditional home and center of worship of the healing hero Asclepius, who, according to the *Naupactica* (an earlier epic, now lost), resurrected the dead Hippolytus and was killed by Zeus as a result. In this tragedy, there is no sign of a potential resurrection and all traces of Asclepius are, literally, invisible.

74. There are many bulls in the myths of Theseus, not least the Minotaur. Bulls are closely associated with male sexuality as well. Thus, this monstrous bull represents the angry sexual jealousy of Theseus, as well as the repressed sexuality of Hippolytus. The bull emerges from the sea, the realm of Aphrodite. See Segal, "The Tragedy of the *Hippolytus:* The Waters of the Ocean and the Untouched Meadow," in Segal (1986), pp. 165–221.

too intricately knotted to escape,[75]
that poor man was dragged along the ground,
his head pounding against the rocks, his body
bashed and bent. His cries would pierce your heart: 1380

"Fillies, raised in my own stables—whoa!
Stop, before you crush me into nothing!
Ah, my father's miserable curse.
Who can come and save the best of men?"

And every one of us wished that we could,   1385
but we were too slow.
                        Then, somehow unsnarled
from those long leather straps, he tumbled free—
I don't know how—still breathing, but just barely.
The fillies disappeared—I don't know where—
the bull did too, that wild portent of grief,   1390
somewhere in that landscape strewn with rocks.

My lord, I am a servant in your house
but there's one thing you can't make me believe:
that your son is a criminal. I don't care
if every woman on earth hangs from a noose   1395
and every pine tree on Mt. Ida[76] falls
to fill the world with letters. I am certain
without a doubt that he is a good man.

CHORUS:
    A new disaster has been brought to pass,
    and there is no release from what must be.   1400

THESEUS:
    Before, I took some pleasure in your words
    out of hatred for the man who met
    this fate. But simple decency, and reverence
    for the gods, and—since he is my son—
    for him, now make me feel neither pleasure   1405
    nor pain at this catastrophe.

75. The way Hippolytus is caught in his reins recalls Phaedra hanging
from her noose.
76. A large wooded mountain near Troy, on which Zeus sits in Homer's
Iliad, watching the warriors battle.

MESSENGER:
                                    What, then?
What would gratify you most? Shall we
bring his broken body in, or do
something else with him? Think carefully:
1410   in my opinion, this is not the time
for cruelty to that unhappy child.

THESEUS:
Bring him in, and let me see his face.
He claims that he has not defiled my bed,
but this god-sent disaster surely proves
1415   that he is lying. That's what I will tell him.

                    (The messenger exits to the left. Theseus remains
                    to await Hippolytus.)

CHORUS:
You, Aphrodite, move what cannot be swayed:
the steely minds of the gods
and of all mankind
rapt beneath the wing of the one who flies with you,
1420   brilliant and sudden. Over the earth he soars;
he skims the tops of the waves
in the echoing surf.
Eros, flashing with gold, in a rush of beating wings
drives every heart insane:
1425   the beasts who dwell in the mountains,
the creatures of the ocean,
all that the earth gives life to,
all the bright sun looks down on,
and every man.
1430   Cypris, you alone
rule over all of these.

                    (Artemis appears above the palace.)

ARTEMIS:
You—
aristocrat, child of Aegeus, I bid you

listen to me: it is I, Leto's daughter,
Artemis speaking.[77]

Theseus, you are pathetic. How could you   1435
take satisfaction in what you have done?
You have killed your own child, a most unholy murder,
putting blind faith in your wife's lying words!
Open your eyes: you are ruined, demolished.

You should pray, in your shame, for the earth to engulf you: 1440
bury your carcass in Tartarus' chasm,[78]
or transform yourself to a bird, with the power
to fly far away from your life full of grief.
The one thing that's clear is that you have no right to
lay claim to the life of a good, decent man.   1445

Listen, Theseus, and hear the full
extent of your misfortunes; though the truth
will clear the way for nothing but your pain.
I've come to let you know how much your son
deserves acclaim in death, for honesty   1450
and virtue, and to tell you how your wife
suffered torment—to show you, in a sense,
her true nobility.
                        She endured the dreadful
choking grip of the goddess we detest
—we who take pleasure in our virginity—   1455
and in that grip your son was her desire.
Phaedra tried to overcome the goddess
by sheer force of her intellect and judgment,
but—much against her will—her nurse's plots

---

77. Theseus has exulted in how Hippolytus' destruction proves that Theseus is the son of Poseidon. But Artemis' choice of address here stresses
that his rash, thoughtless anger marks him as all too human. Aegeus threw
himself off of a cliff when he saw the ship of Theseus with black sails
returning from its mission to Crete. Theseus was supposed to change them
to white if he had been successful in killing the Minotaur. Artemis thus
subtly reminds Theseus that this is not the first time his mistakes have
killed those closest to him. Theseus may be hotheaded and a bad father,
but he does listen to the gods.

78. Tartarus is the lower realm of the Underworld, where sinners such as
Tantalus are punished.

1460   destroyed her, when that woman told your son
        what Phaedra felt, and bound his tongue with oaths.

        Your son did what was right and honorable
        and, naturally, resisted her suggestions;
        and furthermore, he kept his oath, although
1465   it meant enduring your abuse. That man
        is holy; he respects the gods.
                                But Phaedra,
        fearing that the truth would be revealed,
        wrote down lies, destroyed Hippolytus
        with false assertions. Still, you were convinced.

THESEUS:
Oh no.

ARTEMIS:
1470   Does that sting, Theseus? Just wait, and listen
        to what comes next. That's only the beginning
        of your lament. You know that you received
        three potent curses from the ocean-lord,
        your father, and the first of these you used
1475   against your own son, you abomination;
        you might have saved it for an enemy.
        Your father, out of loyalty to you,
        did what he had to do and kept his word.
        But your behavior has offended him
1480   and me; you have revealed yourself as base.
        You wouldn't wait for prophecy, or proof,
        consider solemn pledges, or allow
        measured time to bring in evidence:
        more hastily, more rashly than you should have,
1485   you hurled that deadly curse against your son.

THESEUS:
Mistress, may I die.

ARTEMIS:
                        What you have done
        is ghastly, chilling. Still, you are forgiven
        even for this, perhaps, since it was willed

by Cypris, who made all of these things happen
to satisfy her own offended spirit.   1490

It is not customary for the gods
to interfere with one another's plans;
we let each other's wishes run their course.
If that were not the case, if I did not
respect and fear our father Zeus, believe me,   1495
I never would have let it come to this:
to let him—most beloved of all mortals—
to let him die, to my disgrace.[79]
                                    As for you,
you did wrong, but you were ignorant
of what you did, which mitigates your crime.   1500
Furthermore, your wife, because she died,
removed whatever chance you had to test
the evidence, and this convinced your mind.

This wave of evil crashes down on you
primarily, but I too am affected.   1505
It brings me pain. The gods take no delight
in the death of men who worship and respect them.
But we destroy the wicked utterly:
we crush them, with their houses and their children.

    (Enter Hippolytus carried on a couch by his
    attendants.)[80]

CHORUS:
    Look—
    here comes the unfortunate victim, who once had   1510
    such a strong, youthful body, such fine chestnut hair;
    now he is mangled and gashed, and the household

---

79. Artemis claims that Zeus does not allow the gods to tangle in each
other's plans with respect to mortals. Instead, they respond afterward,
with disaster for still more humans, as Artemis is to pledge shortly
(1583–90).

80. This entrance is one of the striking structural symmetries in this
drama, for the weak, dying, supine Hippolytus now clearly resembles
Phaedra in her first appearance. Recall here how Phaedra's final speech
ended with the promise that he will share in her illness (809).

must labor beneath this new burden of pain:
this attack of the gods, this incursion of sorrow.

HIPPOLYTUS:

> *(Cries aloud in pain.)*

1515   Ah, my horrible fate, and my impious father;
his immoral prayers to the gods, his injustice
have mangled my body. I am destroyed.
Arrows of pain and unbearable spasms
are darting like fire in my brain and my skull.
1520   Let me rest—wait a minute—I can't keep on going.

> *(They pause for a moment; when Hippolytus
> moves again, the acute pain returns.)*

Aaaaaaah!

Hateful chariot, team that I raised myself,
you have torn me to pieces, reduced me to shreds.

Oohh! Please, by the gods, be more gentle, my servants:
watch how you touch me; don't press on my wounds.
1525   Who is it there on my right? Take it easy:
raise my body a little, support me more firmly,
accursèd and blasted by fate as I am,
called down to my death by the miscalculation
of my misguided father.
                              Zeus, Zeus, do you see this?
1530   It is I, who have always been better than others,
more reverent and worshipful; I, who have never
been equaled on earth for my wise restraint—I
who now approach Hades with eyes staring open,
life lying broken, and all of my piety
1535   wasted, my efforts, my labors of kindness—
it's no use.

> *(Hippolytus cries aloud again. Here he shifts from
> chanting to singing.)*

The pain overtakes me. Agony, agony.
Please, let me go, let Death come and heal me,

destroy me, destroy me. I'm longing to feel
the edge of a blade that will shear through my body,   1540
cut through me completely and lay me to rest.

Miserable curse of my father! Some ancient
blood-crime, ancestral pollution, has broken
out of its boundaries, erupted on us.

It comes to me, but I do not know why.   1545
I'm innocent; I have done nothing.

Sorrow, sorrow.
There's nothing I can say.
I don't know how to leave my pain behind.

Dark Hades, take me in your arms;   1550
carry me down to the final, enfolding
certainty of night.

ARTEMIS:
Poor man, entwined so tightly in disaster,
destroyed by your nobility of mind.

HIPPOLYTUS:
Ah!
The fragrance of the goddess. Even now   1555
my shattered body senses the relief
of your sweet exhalation, Artemis—
Artemis is somewhere close at hand.

ARTEMIS:
Poor man, I *am* here. Your beloved goddess.

HIPPOLYTUS:
Mistress, do you see how I am broken?   1560

ARTEMIS:
Yes.
But it would not be right for me to weep.

HIPPOLYTUS:
Your servant in the hunt exists no more . . .

ARTEMIS:
And yet I love you, though you are destroyed.

HIPPOLYTUS:
. . . guardian of your horses and your statue.

ARTEMIS:
1565   Cypris plotted this outrageous crime.

HIPPOLYTUS:
Ah. Now I know the power that destroyed me.

ARTEMIS:
You slighted her—and your restraint was wise.
That's why she hated you.

HIPPOLYTUS:
                              A single goddess
has utterly destroyed the three of us.

ARTEMIS:
1570   Yes: you, your father, and your father's wife.

HIPPOLYTUS:
My father. Yes. I grieve for him as well.

ARTEMIS:
He was deceived, as part of Cypris' plan.

HIPPOLYTUS:
Unhappy father, caught in this disaster.

THESEUS:
My child, I am destroyed. I can no longer
take delight in life.

HIPPOLYTUS:
1575   The thing you did
was wrong. I weep for you more than for me.

THESEUS:
If only I could die instead of you.

HIPPOLYTUS:
  The gifts your father gave you were most bitter.

THESEUS:
  I wish that curse had never left my lips.

HIPPOLYTUS:
  But you would have killed me anyway! You were angry.   1580

THESEUS:
  True; the gods had robbed me of my sense.

HIPPOLYTUS:

  (Groans indignantly.)

  If only mortal men could curse the gods!⁸¹

ARTEMIS:
  You've said enough.
              Don't worry: Cypris' plans,
  her anger, which has splintered your poor body,
  will not go unpunished, though you dwell   1585
  in the gloom beneath the earth. I shall reward
  your piety, your uncorrupted mind.
  And I'll exact a price from Aphrodite:
  these arrows, which are inescapable,
  will strike whatever mortal she loves most.⁸²   1590

  For you, unhappy man, to compensate
  your suffering, I shall establish here

---

81. In Greek tragedy, the central characters typically have a moment
when they realize and openly acknowledge that they have been wrong.
Such a recognition is often a turning point in the action. But at no point
does Hippolytus make any such concession; he approaches death full of
rage and resentment.

82. The victim she has in mind is almost certainly Adonis, the beautiful
human lover of Aphrodite, who dies during a boar hunt. Humans are thus
collateral damage in the wars between the gods. As Gloucester says in
King Lear, "As flies to wanton boys are we to the gods / they kill us for
their sport" (IV.i.36–37).

the greatest honor possible: young girls
of Troezen, when their time has come to marry,
1595   will cut their hair in sacrifice to you,
and you will reap the fruit of all their tears
and all their boundless sorrow, through the ages.
For all of time young virgins will compose
and sing their songs for you, and Phaedra's love
1600   will not be veiled in silence; her desire
for you will be well-known throughout the land.[83]

Theseus, son of elderly Aegeus,
embrace your child now, and hold him close.
You killed him without knowing what you did,
1605   and human beings are likely to go wrong
when they have gods to help them.
                              As for you,
Hippolytus, do not despise your father.
You were cut down by your own destiny.

And now, farewell. It is not right for me
1610   to look upon the dying, to defile
my vision with a mortal's final gasp.
And I can see that you are close to death.

(Exit Artemis.)

HIPPOLYTUS:
Immortal virgin, I bid you farewell.
The gods are truly blessed. How easily
1615   you take your leave of me, and our long friendship.[84]
Because you ask me to, I'll put an end

---

83. Hippolytus was in fact worshiped in cult, but Artemis' promise to
Hippolytus, that he will be honored by girls and forever linked in song
with Phaedra's desire, does not seem to conform to what he might choose.
The cutting of hair is a sign of mourning on two levels: one, mourning for
Hippolytus, and, second, for the girls themselves as their younger selves
die and are reborn as wives after marriage.

84. Another angry and resentful accusation? Or a simple acknowledgment and acceptance of the distance between mortals and gods? One
should keep in mind here that Artemis, literally, is distant, high above Hippolytus and his father.

to my grievance with my father. In the past
I have always done what you have wanted.

Ah! The darkness steals into my eyes.
Death is coming. Take me in your arms,   1620
keep my body straight. It's time now, Father.

THESEUS:
   Oh, child, how can you do this? Oh, misfortune.

HIPPOLYTUS:
   I am destroyed. I see the gates of Hades.

THESEUS:
   You're leaving me. Your blood is on my hands.

HIPPOLYTUS:
   No, Father. I absolve you of this murder.   1625

THESEUS:
   Really? You would clear me of your blood-guilt?

HIPPOLYTUS:
   I call as witness Artemis the huntress.

THESEUS:
   My own dear son, how nobly you have acted.

HIPPOLYTUS:
   Farewell, Father. A fond farewell to you.

THESEUS:
   Oh, god. Your pious, uncorrupted mind!   1630

HIPPOLYTUS:
   Father, pray that your legitimate
   sons may be so good.

THESEUS:
                  Please, don't betray me
   now, my child! You must hold on, endure!

HIPPOLYTUS:
I have endured my last. I am destroyed.
1635   Hurry now, and cover up my face.[85]

THESEUS:
Glorious Athens, dominion of the goddess
Pallas Athena, what a man you have lost.

Cypris, I will not forget the power
of your great harm, and my unhappiness.

(Exit Theseus and attendants bearing Hippolytus'
body into the palace.)

CHORUS:
1640   We all share this grief.
Every citizen mourns.
This was so unexpected—
an unforeseen shock.
Volleys of tears
1645   will descend for this tale.
Great is the outcry
lamenting the great.

(Exit the Chorus and remaining attendants to the
right.)

---

85. The covering of Hippolytus' body in death echoes the play with Phaedra's veil as she lay on her sickbed (223–64).

Endnotes and Comments on the Text

In the notes below I have translated, for the sake of completeness, lines that appear in the manuscripts of Euripides but are not considered genuine by modern editors, who mark such lines as probable interpolations by putting them in square brackets. Additions to the text after Euripides' lifetime may have been made by actors (Euripides' plays were performed often in the centuries following his death) or by scribes copying the texts; the earliest manuscripts we have of Euripides' plays are from the Middle Ages and reflect many stages of copying and recopying. An actor might insert a line or passage from another play to please the audience; similarly, a scribe might copy a "parallel passage" into the margin of his text, which a later copyist might insert into the text itself. On the history of the texts, see Barrett (1964), pp. 45–90; Page (1971), pp. xxxvii–lvii; and Csapo and Slater (1995), pp. 1–38.

I have also noted lines that I have kept in the text in spite of editors' objections (it seems to me not impossible that Euripides himself would repeat a line or phrase), and pointed out some patterns of language in the Greek (see notes ix, xv, and xvi on *Medea*).

—DAS

Alcestis

i. There is probably a lacuna (something missing from the manuscripts) after this line, 204 of the Greek text. This was first proposed by Elmsley.

ii. The manuscripts give another line after this (208 of the Greek):

see the sun's great circle, and its blaze.

However, lines 207–8 of the Greek (211 of my translation = 207) are nearly identical to *Hecuba* 411–12 (where the verb is first person rather than third). Some editors delete both lines here, some only the second, as I have done. One or both lines apparently intruded into the text after being copied into the margin as a parallel passage. See Dale (1954, *ad loc.*).

iii. The rest of this line (226 of the Greek) is missing.

iv. Here I omit line 312 of the Greek, "to speak to and to listen in return," which is nearly identical to line 195 (cf. line 196 in my translation). It doesn't fit well here and is bracketed by most editors to indicate that it doesn't belong in the text.

v. Some of the text seems to be missing here, or possibly elsewhere in the ode. The strophe and antistrophe do not correspond in length.

vi. Evidently a line is missing here.

vii. The exact translation is uncertain here, and a few syllables seem to be missing from the text (line 594 of the Greek).

viii. Here I omit lines 651–52 of the Greek:

> We could have lived our days out, she and I,
> and I would not be moaning now, bereaved.

These lines, a near-repetition of 295–96 (313–14 in my translation), seem to have wrongly crept into the text here, where most editors agree they are intrusive.

ix. Editors suspect these two half-lines ("Fling your cares aside, / put garlands on your head!" 795–96 of the Greek) as an interpolation because very similar phrases occur in lines 829 and 832 of the Greek (see 877 and 880 in my translation).

x. I omit the following three lines, 818–20 of the Greek:

> SERVANT:
>> We're grieving. You can see our hair is shorn,
>> our robes are black.
>
> HERACLES:
>>   Who died? It surely wasn't
>> one of the children? Or was it his old father?

These lines are not considered genuine by editors, based on a combination of formal features and an ancient commentator's note that these lines did not appear in all manuscripts. See Dale's commentary (1954, *ad loc.*).

xi. These last six lines (in chanted anapests) are also found at the end of four other plays by Euripides: *Andromache, Helen, Bacchae,* and *Medea.* In *Medea,* there is a small variation: the first line, 1463 in my translation, mentions Zeus the enforcer (cf. 171) instead of "the deities." We do not know whether Euripides himself ended each of these plays with this coda, or if it was added by actors or editors. For the latter view, see Mastronarde (2002) on *Medea* 1415–19. For the former, in the case of *Medea*, and a defense of the significance of Zeus in the variation, see Kovacs (1987), pp. 268–70, and (1993). On codas in Sophocles and Euripides, see Roberts (1987).

Medea

i. I have omitted the following line (41 in the Greek text): "creeping silently into their bedroom." See Willink (1988) for the deletion of this line and a defense of the surrounding lines. Compare line 387 (379 in the Greek) and note vii below.

ii. The following line (87 in the Greek text) was condemned by ancient commentators, and modern editors continue to reject it as intrusive:

Some with good reason, some for the sake of gain.

iii. I retain this line, 246 in the Greek (reading Porson's *hêlikas* to solve the metrical problem), though most editors, following Wilamowitz, reject it as an interpolation. See Podlecki (1989) and Mastronarde (2002), *ad loc.*

iv. I omit the following line, 262 in the Greek:

the daughter whom he married, and her father.

Most editors follow Lenting (1820) in deleting this as an interpolation based on line 288 (295 in my translation). The Greek is unidiomatic, and the line is distracting and ineffective.

v. I retain this line (304 in the Greek), although it was deleted by Pierson (1752) and is still considered an interpolation by most editors, in part because of its similarity to line 808 of the Greek (830 in my translation).

vi. See Kovacs (1987), pp. 267–68, on the text of lines 357–61 of the Greek (366–69 of my translation).

vii. I omit the following line:

or thrust a sharpened knife-blade through the liver

See Willink (1988), and compare line 47 of the translation (40 of the Greek text), and note i above.

viii. The same line (468 of the Greek text) is found at 1324 (1369–70 in my translation), where Jason flings it back at Medea after calling her "most detested." Most editors (following Brunck, 1779) delete the line here; see Mastronarde's (2002) commentary on 468. In my view, the line is appropriate in both contexts.

ix. With the phrase "saved your life" (cf. 481 above), Medea brings her argument to a close. This technique of beginning and ending with the same words (ring composition) is used on a smaller scale in Jason's speech above, with the words "You are now an exile" (453, 464).

x. The following line ("to the bride, to be exempt from exile," 785 in the Greek), omitted here, is grammatically awkward. It is not present in all manuscripts, and most editors (since Valckenaer) have rejected it.

xi. I omit the following two lines, 1006–7 in the Greek text:

Why have you turned your face away? Why aren't you
happy to hear what I have had to say?

They are repeated almost exactly from 923–24 (946–49 in my translation). See Mastronarde (2002, *ad loc.*).

xii. Lines 1062–63 omitted:

They must die anyway, and since they must,
I will kill them. I'm the one who bore them.

These lines are also found in the manuscripts at 1240–41 (1264–65 English), where they fit the context better.

xiii. Reading *tolmêsô*, with the majority of the manuscripts, in line 1078 of the Greek.

xiv. The preceding line ("You who have done this terrible lawless deed," 1121 of the Greek text), omitted here, is missing from some of the manuscripts, and many editors have deleted it, following Lenting (1820).

xv. Euripides here uses a verb that means both "destroyed" and "lost," and that punctuates the sections of Jason's speech; it occurs at the end of line 1326 of the Greek (*apôlesas*, "you have destroyed"; 1372 English), and twelve lines later at 1338 (*apôlesas* again; 1386 English); his speech ends another twelve lines later with *apôlesa*, "I've lost" (1350; 1398 English). The effect of this patterned repetition and the double meaning of *apôlesa* ("I have destroyed") is striking. Jason uses the verb again at 1365 (1414 English).

This verb is frequent in Euripides, and Aristophanes may have been making fun of (among other things) the tragedian's fondness for it in the *lêkythion apôlesen* scene of *Frogs* (1208 ff). The character Aeschylus ridicules the character Euripides by completing several of his verses with this phrase, which means "lost his little oil jar."

xvi. The play ends as it began, with a character wishing that all this had never happened: the Nurse, line 1, *Eith' ôphel'... mê...*; here, *mêpot'... ophelon*, 1413 (1463 English).

xvii. On these last six lines, see note xi on *Alcestis* 1228.

Hippolytus

i. Lines 625–26 of the Greek omitted:

But as it is, a man must pay out cash
to bring this evil thing into his house.

For this omission and others in this play, see Barrett's commentary (1964). These lines, which refer to the older custom of paying a "bride price" to a woman's father, are inconsistent with the following lines, which refer to the contemporary custom of the father's paying a dowry (689–91 English, 628–29 Greek). An interpolator may have inserted the "bride price" lines as a correction of the perceived anachronism of the dowry reference, since the play is set in the heroic past. As Barrett points out (*ad loc.*), Euripides "was indifferent to such anachronisms and commits them by the score." See, for example, the note at *Alcestis* 715. Lines 625–26 were first deleted by Nauck (1854).

ii. Lines 634–37 of the Greek omitted:

He's forced into it. He might marry well—
his in-laws a delight, his wife like hell—
or he might love his bride but find her parents
distress him past the limits of endurance.
He uses what he can to bind his wounds.

These lines do not fit the context, and editors since Barthold (1885) have deleted them. They may have been inserted by an actor, as Barrett argues (1964, *ad loc.*).

iii. Line 663 omitted:

I'll know that I have felt your shamelessness.

iv. This song (669–79 Greek; 734–50 English) is traditionally assigned to Phaedra, and some modern editors, including Barrett (1964) and Diggle (1984), give it to her. Smith (1960) first argued that these words are more appropriate for the Nurse, and Østerud (1970) has made this case fully and persuasively; they are followed by Kovacs (1995/2005) in his Loeb Classical Library edition.

v. I omit the translation of the corrupt line and a half at 867–68 of the Greek. The text of the manuscripts here is hopelessly garbled.

vi. I omit the next three lines:

Dear god, don't make this house pay such a price.
Please hear my prayer. I have a prophet's vision:
birds of ill omen circling overhead.

These lines (871–73 in the Greek) were missing from some of the ancient manuscripts, and most editors do not consider them genuine.

vii. There are textual difficulties with lines 1142–45 (1012–15 of the Greek), and Barrett (1964) and others have suspected all or part of this passage as an interpolation. Line 1144 (1014 Greek) has been judged illogical and therefore corrupt by most editors, with the phrase "not at all, unless" raising the most suspicion. Barrett emended "unless (*ei mê*)" to "because/since (*epei*)." A more literal translation of 1144 (1014), accepting Barrett's emendation, is "Not at all, since kingly power has corrupted the minds of all those who love it" (Kovacs 1995/2005).

viii. Line 1029 omitted:

a wandering exile with no home or city

ix. Line 1050 omitted:

A man who's evil gets what he has earned.

Select Bibliography

This (very selective) list focuses on relatively recent scholarship written in English, which is for the most part available in good university libraries. When important articles have been republished in prominent collections of essays, only the new publication information is cited.

Editions, Commentaries, and Textual Discussions

Allen, James T., and Gabriel Italie, eds. *A Concordance to Euripides*. Berkeley and London: University of California Press and Cambridge University Press, 1954.

Barrett, W. S., ed. and comm. *Euripides:* Hippolytos. Oxford: Clarendon Press, 1964.

Conacher, D. J., ed., trans., and comm. *Euripides:* Alcestis. Warminster: Aris and Phillips, 1988.

Dale, A. M., ed. and comm. *Euripides:* Alcestis. Oxford: Clarendon Press, 1954.

Diggle, J., ed. *Euripidis Fabulae*. Vol. 1. New York: Oxford University Press, 1984.

Halleran, Michael R., trans. and comm. *Euripides:* Hippolytus. Warminster: Aris and Phillips, 1995.

Kovacs, David. "Treading the Circle Warily: Literary Criticism and the Text of Euripides." *Transactions of the American Philological Association* 117 (1987): 257–70.

———, ed. and trans. *Euripides I:* Cyclops, Alcestis, Medea. Cambridge, MA: Harvard University Press, 1994. Repr. with corrections 2001.

———, ed. and trans. *Euripides II:* Children of Heracles, Hippolytus, Andromache, Hecuba. Cambridge, MA: Harvard University Press, 1995. Repr. with revisions and corrections 2005.

Mastronarde, Donald J., ed. and comm. *Euripides:* Medea. New York: Cambridge University Press, 2002.

Østerud, Svein. "Who Sings the Monody 669–79 in Euripides' *Hippolytus?*" *Greek, Roman and Byzantine Studies* 11 (1970): 307–20.

Page, Denys L. *Euripides:* Medea. Oxford: Clarendon Press, 1938. Repr. with corrections 1971.

Podlecki, Anthony J., trans. and comm. *Euripides'* Medea. Newburyport, MA: Focus Classical Library, 1989.

Roberts, Deborah H. "Parting Words: Final Lines in Sophocles and Euripides." *Classical Quarterly* 37 (1987): 51–64.

Roisman, H. M., and C. A. E. Luschnig, eds. and comm. *Euripides' Alcestis*. Norman: University of Oklahoma Press, 2003.

Smith, W. D. "Staging the Central Scene of the *Hippolytus*." *Transactions of the American Philological Association* 91 (1960): 162–77.

Willink, C. W. "Eur. *Medea* 1–45, 371–85." *Classical Quarterly* 38 (1988): 313–23.

Works on Greek Theater and Society

Arrowsmith, William. "A Greek Theater of Ideas." In Erich Segal, ed. (1968), pp. 13–33.

Belfiore, Elizabeth S. *Murder among Friends: Violation of* Philia *in Greek Tragedy*. New York: Oxford University Press, 2000.

Buxton, R. G. A. *Persuasion in Greek Tragedy: A Study of* Peitho. New York: Cambridge University Press, 1982.

Cairns, Douglas L. Aidôs: *The Psychology and Ethics of Honour and Shame in Ancient Greek Literature*. Oxford: Oxford University Press, 1993.

Csapo, Eric, and William J. Slater. *The Context of Ancient Drama*. Ann Arbor: University of Michigan Press, 1995.

Easterling, P. E., ed. *The Cambridge Companion to Greek Tragedy*. Cambridge: Cambridge University Press, 1997.

Easterling, P. E., and Bernard Knox, eds. *The Cambridge History of Classical Literature*. Vol. I, *Greek Literature*. Cambridge: Cambridge University Press, 1985.

Foley, Helene P. "Modern Performance and Adaptation of Greek Tragedy." *Transactions of the American Philological Association* 129 (1999): 1–12.

———. *Female Acts in Greek Tragedy*. Princeton, NJ: Princeton University Press, 2001.

Golder, Herbert, and Stephen Scully, eds. "The Chorus in Greek Tragedy and Culture." *Arion* 3.1 and 4.1 (1994–96).

Goldhill, Simon. *Reading Greek Tragedy*. Cambridge: Cambridge University Press, 1986.

———. "The Great Dionysia and Civic Ideology." In John J. Winkler and Froma I. Zeitlin, eds. (1990), pp. 97–129.

Goldhill, Simon, and Robin Osborne, eds. *Performance Culture and Athenian Democracy*. Cambridge: Cambridge University Press, 1999.

Gregory, Justina, ed. *A Companion to Greek Tragedy.* Malden, MA: Blackwell, 2005.

Griffin, Jasper. "The Social Function of Attic Tragedy." *Classical Quarterly* 48 (1998): 39–61.

Hall, Edith. *Inventing the Barbarian: Greek Self-Definition through Tragedy.* New York: Oxford University Press, 1989.

Henderson, J. "Women and the Athenian Dramatic Festivals." *Transactions of the American Philological Association* 121 (1991): 133–47.

Jones, John. *On Aristotle and Greek Tragedy.* London: Chatto and Windus, 1962.

Knox, Bernard. *Word and Action: Essays on the Ancient Theater.* Baltimore, MD: Johns Hopkins University Press, 1979.

Lefkowitz, Mary. *The Lives of the Greek Poets.* Baltimore, MD: Johns Hopkins University Press, 1981.

Lesky, Albin. *Greek Tragic Poetry.* Translated by Matthew Dillon. New Haven, CT: Yale University Press, 1983.

McClure, Laura. *Spoken Like a Woman: Speech and Gender in Athenian Drama.* Princeton, NJ: Princeton University Press, 1999.

Mitchell-Boyask, Robin. *Plague and the Athenian Imagination: Drama, History, and the Cult of Asclepius.* Cambridge: Cambridge University Press, 2007.

Nussbaum, Martha. *The Fragility of Goodness: Luck and Ethics in Greek Tragedy and Philosophy.* Cambridge: Cambridge University Press, 1986.

Rehm, Rush. *Greek Tragic Theatre.* New York: Routledge, 1992.

———. *Marriage to Death: The Conflation of Wedding and Funeral Rituals in Greek Tragedy.* Princeton, NJ: Princeton University Press, 1994.

Seaford, Richard. "The Social Function of Attic Tragedy: A Response to Jasper Griffin." *Classical Quarterly* 50 (2000): 30–44.

Segal, Charles. *Interpreting Greek Tragedy: Myth, Poetry, Text.* Ithaca, NY: Cornell University Press, 1986.

Silk, M. S., ed. *Tragedy and the Tragic: Greek Theatre and Beyond.* Oxford: Oxford University Press, 1996.

Strauss, Barry S. *Fathers and Sons in Athens: Ideology and Society in the Era of the Peloponnesian War.* Princeton, NJ: Princeton University Press, 1993.

Taplin, Oliver. *Greek Tragedy in Action.* Berkeley: University of California Press, 1978.

Vernant, Jean-Pierre, and Pierre Vidal-Naquet. *Myth and Tragedy in Ancient Greece.* Translated by Janet Lloyd. New York: Zone Books, 1988.

Wiles, David. *Tragedy in Athens: Performance Space and Theatrical Meaning*. New York: Cambridge University Press, 1997.

Winkler, John J., and Froma I. Zeitlin, eds. *Nothing to Do with Dionysos? Athenian Drama in Its Social Context*. Princeton, NJ: Princeton University Press, 1990.

Wohl, Victoria. *Intimate Commerce: Exchange, Gender, and Subjectivity in Greek Tragedy*. Austin: University of Texas Press, 1998.

Zeitlin, Froma I. *Playing the Other: Gender and Society in Classical Greek Literature*. Chicago: University of Chicago Press, 1996.

General Works on Euripides

Arnott, W. G. "Euripides and the Unexpected." *Greece and Rome* 20 (1984): 49–64.

Barlow, Shirley A. *The Imagery of Euripides: A Study in the Dramatic Use of Pictorial Language*. 2nd ed. Bristol: Bristol Classical Press, 1986.

Burian, Peter, ed. *Directions in Euripidean Criticism*. Durham, NC: Duke University Press, 1985.

Collard, Christopher. *Euripides*. Greece and Rome: New Surveys in the Classics, 14. Oxford: Clarendon Press, 1981.

Conacher, D. J. *Euripidean Drama: Myth, Theme and Structure*. Toronto: University of Toronto Press, 1967.

Dunn, Francis M. *Tragedy's End: Closure and Innovation in Euripidean Drama*. New York: Oxford University Press, 1996.

Fletcher, Judith. "Women and Oaths in Euripides." *Theatre Journal* 55 (2003): 29–44.

Foley, Helene P. *Ritual Irony: Poetry and Sacrifice in Euripides*. Ithaca, NY: Cornell University Press, 1985.

Gregory, Justina. *Euripides and the Instruction of the Athenians*. Ann Arbor: University of Michigan Press, 1991.

———. "Euripides as Social Critic." *Greece and Rome* 49 (2002): 145–62.

Halleran, Michael R. *The Stagecraft in Euripides*. London: Croom Helm, 1985.

Meltzer, Gary S. *Euripides and the Poetics of Nostalgia*. Cambridge: Cambridge University Press, 2006.

Michelini, Ann N. *Euripides and the Tragic Tradition*. Madison: University of Wisconsin Press, 1987.

Mitchell-Boyask, Robin, ed. *Approaches to Teaching the Dramas of Euripides*. New York: Modern Language Association of America, 2002.

Mossman, Judith, ed. *Oxford Readings in Classical Studies: Euripides.* New York: Oxford University Press, 2003.

Powell, Anton, ed. *Euripides, Women, and Sexuality.* London and New York: Routledge, 1990.

Rabinowitz, Nancy Sorkin. *Anxiety Veiled: Euripides and the Traffic in Women.* Ithaca, NY: Cornell University Press, 1993.

Sansone, David. "Plato and Euripides." *Illinois Classical Studies* 21 (1996): 35–61.

Scullion, S. "Euripides and Macedon, or the Silence of the Frogs." *Classical Quarterly* 53 (2003): 389–400.

Segal, Charles. *Euripides and the Poetics of Sorrow: Art, Gender, and Commemoration in* Alcestis, Hippolytus, *and* Hecuba. Durham, NC: Duke University Press, 1993.

Segal, Erich, ed. *Euripides: A Collection of Critical Essays.* Englewood Cliffs, NJ: Prentice-Hall, 1968.

Winnington-Ingram, R. P. "Euripides: *Poietes Sophos.*" In Judith Mossman, ed. (2003), pp. 47–63.

Studies of *Alcestis*

Beye, Charles R. "Alcestis and Her Critics." *Greek, Roman and Byzantine Studies* 2 (1959): 109–27.

Burnett, A. "The Virtues of Admetus." In Erich Segal, ed. (1968), pp. 51–69.

Buxton, R. G. A. "Euripides' *Alkestis:* Five Aspects of an Interpretation." In Judith Mossman, ed. (2003), pp. 170–86.

Dyson, M. "Alcestis' Children and the Character of Admetus." *Journal of Hellenic Studies* 108 (1988): 13–23.

Garner, R. "Death and Victory in Euripides' *Alcestis.*" *Classical Antiquity* 7 (1988): 58–71.

Lloyd, M. "Euripides' *Alcestis.*" *Greece and Rome* 32 (1985): 119–31.

Marshall, C. W. "*Alcestis* and the Problem of Prosatyric Drama." *Classical Journal* 95 (2000): 229–38.

Murnaghan, Sheila. "The Survivors' Song: The Drama of Mourning in Euripides' *Alcestis.*" *Illinois Classical Studies* 24–25 (1999–2000): 107–16.

O'Higgins, Dolores. "Above Rubies: Admetus' Perfect Wife." *Arethusa* 26 (1993): 77–97.

Padilla, Mark W. "Gifts of Humiliation: *Charis* and Tragic Experience in *Alcestis.*" *American Journal of Philology* 121 (2000): 179–211.

Slater, N. "Dead Again: (En)gendering Praise in Euripides' *Alcestis*." *Helios* 27 (2000): 105–21.

Wilson, John R., ed. *Twentieth Century Interpretations of Euripides' Alcestis*. Englewood Cliffs, NJ: Prentice-Hall, 1968.

(See also chapters in Conacher 1967, Dunn, Foley 2001, Gregory 1991, Mitchell-Boyask 2002, Rabinowitz, Rehm 1994, C. Segal 1993, and Wohl.)

Studies of *Medea*

Allan, William. *Euripides:* Medea. Duckworth Companions to Greek and Roman Tragedy. London: Duckworth, 2002.

Barlow, S. A. "Stereotype and Reversal in Euripides' *Medea*." *Greece and Rome* 36 (1989): 158–71.

Boedeker, Deborah. "Euripides' *Medea* and the Vanity of *Logoi*." *Classical Philology* 86 (1991): 95–112.

Burnett, Anne. "Medea and the Tragedy of Revenge." *Classical Philology* 68 (1973): 1–24.

Clauss, James J., and Sarah Iles Johnston, eds. *Medea: Essays on Medea in Myth, Literature, Philosophy, and Art*. Princeton, NJ: Princeton University Press, 1997.

Easterling, P. E. "The Infanticide in Euripides' *Medea*." In Judith Mossman, ed. (2003), pp. 187–200.

Gellrich, Michelle. "Medea Hypokrites." *Arethusa* 35 (2002): 315–37.

Hall, Edith, Fiona Macintosh, and Oliver Taplin, eds. *Medea in Performance 1500–2000*. Oxford: Legenda, 2000.

Kovacs, David. "Zeus in Euripides' *Medea*." *American Journal of Philology* 114 (1993): 45–70.

McDermott, Emily A. *Euripides' Medea: The Incarnation of Disorder*. University Park: Pennsylvania State University Press, 1989.

Mueller, Melissa. "The Language of Reciprocity in Euripides' *Medea*." *American Journal of Philology* 122 (2001): 471–504.

Sfyroeras, P. "The Ironies of Salvation: The Aigeus Scene in Euripides' *Medea*." *Classical Journal* 90 (1995): 125–42.

(See also chapters in Dunn, Foley 2001, Knox, Mitchell-Boyask 2002, Rabinowitz, and Rehm 1994. For a more detailed bibliography, see Allan.)

Studies of *Hippolytus*

Arnson Svarlien, Diane. "A Translator's Notebook: The Third Stasimon of Euripides' *Hippolytus*." In Richard Armstrong and Elizabeth Vandiver, eds., *Remusings; Classical and Modern Literature* 27.1 (2007). *Remusings* collection also forthcoming as an online book from the Center for Hellenic Studies (www.chs.harvard.edu).

Burian, Peter. "Myth into *Mythos*: The Shaping of Tragic Plot." In P. E. Easterling, ed. (1997), pp. 178–210.

Cairns, Douglas L. "The Meadow of Artemis and the Character of the Euripidean Hippolytus." *Quaderni urbinati di cultura classica* 57 (1997): 51–75.

Gibert, J. C. "Euripides' Hippolytus Plays: Which Came First." *Classical Quarterly* 47 (1997): 85–97.

Goff, Barbara. *The Noose of Words: Readings of Desire, Violence, and Language in Euripides'* Hippolytos. New York: Cambridge University Press, 1990.

Kovacs, David. *The Heroic Muse: Studies in the* Hippolytus *and the* Hecuba *of Euripides*. Baltimore, MD: Johns Hopkins University Press, 1987.

Mills, Sophie. *Euripides:* Hippolytus. Duckworth Companions to Greek and Roman Tragedy. London: Duckworth, 2002.

Mitchell-Boyask, Robin N. "Euripides' *Hippolytus* and the Trials of Manhood (The *Ephebia?*)." In Mark W. Padilla, ed., *Rites of Passage in Ancient Greece: Literature, Religion, Society*. Lewisburg, PA: Bucknell University Press, 1999, pp. 42–66.

Reckford, K. "Phaethon, Hippolytus, and Aphrodite." *Transactions of the American Philological Association* 103 (1972): 414–16.

———. "Phaedra and Pasiphae: The Pull Backward." *Transactions of the American Philological Association* 104 (1974): 307–28.

Roisman, Hanna. *Nothing Is as It Seems: The Tragedy of the Implicit in Euripides'* Hippolytus. Lanham, MD: Rowman and Littlefield, 1999.

Winnington-Ingram, R. P. "Hippolytus: A Study in Causation." In Judith Mossman, ed. (2003), pp. 218–60.

Woodruff, Paul. *Reverence: Renewing a Forgotten Virtue*. New York: Oxford University Press, 2001.

(See also chapters in Dunn, Gregory 1991, Knox, McClure, Meltzer, Michelini, Mitchell-Boyask 2002, Rabinowitz, C. Segal 1986 and 1993, E. Segal, Strauss, and Zeitlin. For a more detailed bibliography, see Mills.)